Increaible Command

Paul H. Eldridge

Pacific Press Publishing Association
Boise, Idaho
Oshawa, Ontario, Canada

Edited by Don Mansell
Designed by Tim Larson
Cover Illustration by Darrel Tank
Type set in 10/12 Century Schoolbook

Copyright © 1988 by
Pacific Press Publishing Association
Printed in United States of America
All Rights Reserved

Library of Congress Catalog Card Number: 88-60599

ISBN 0-8163-0748-2

88 89 90 91 92 • 5 4 3 2 1

Contents

Incredible Command	5
The Path of Simplicity	
Shoes, Wheels, or Wings?	13
Winsome Magnetism	21
The Path of Supplication	
"Give Us This Day . . ."	31
Heaven—Earth: Direct Communication Connection	38
Un-natural Resources	45
The Path of Self-Denial	
Watch Out for Number One	55
Giving Up, or Giving In—Why?	61
The Path of Service	
Whose Priorities?	73
God Wants *You!*	80
The Path of Suffering	
Pain Threshold, Endurance Limit	89
"Why Me, Lord?"	97
The Path of Sacrifice	
Love Without Limit	105
"With His Stripes We are Healed"	110
The Path of Satisfaction	
Satisfaction Guaranteed	119

Chapter 1
Incredible Command

The burly fisherman stood, and as the boat swayed, he spread his legs with a loose-kneed stance against the motion of the water. His gnarled hands seized the rough cord of the fishing net. Then he and his brother, instinctively coordinating their movements with practiced skill, tossed the net out into the waters of the Sea of Galilee.

The results were spectacular!

Suddenly the waters churned with thrashing fish. Peter and his brother Andrew, faced with the biggest catch of their lives, fought with total concentration to haul the net aboard. Unable to handle it by themselves, they shouted for their partners, James and John, to come and help.

Finally, by working together, the fishermen succeeded in dragging the huge catch to shore. Without trying to understand their excitement, their minds reviewed the whole incredible episode.

It had begun earlier that morning. Coming ashore from an unsuccessful night on the lake, they had met Jesus of Nazareth, the strange new teacher. He had commandeered Peter's boat, and, using it as a podium, had spoken to the crowd that had quickly gathered. Then, His brief sermon finished, Jesus had suggested another attempt at fishing.

"We have toiled all the night, and have taken nothing," Peter had replied. "Nevertheless, at Thy word I will let down the net."

Then it had happened—this unbelievable catch!

6 INCREDIBLE COMMAND

And now, once more they listened to Jesus' voice. He spoke with friendliness, but also with authority. Puzzled and intrigued, they heard Him say, "Follow Me, and I will make you fishers of men."

Something about the tone of His voice, something about His personality left them no alternative. They must obey.

Just a few steps away, James and John were working with Zebedee, their father, mending the nets. Once more Jesus spoke.

"Follow Me."

James and John turned their backs on their business, leaving their father with the boat and the nets—and the amazing catch of fishes. Joining Peter and Andrew, they walked after this magnetic new Teacher, down the shores of Galilee, and into the pages of sacred history. They became His first disciples. Matthew 4:19-22; Luke 5:1-11.

These men, who to outward appearances lacked the qualifications for effective leadership, obeyed Jesus' command—and were never the same again. Their lives were completely and permanently transformed as they moved out in obedience to the Incredible Command: "Follow Me." Others since then have obeyed the same command and have experienced the same results.

Jesus Speaks to You

Those remarkable words with which Jesus summoned His first followers have never been rescinded. Every individual who has ever had an encounter with Him has been confronted by the same command.

And the Voice that says, "Follow Me," is modulated to every individual circumstance. It comes as an answer to every desire for a better life, at every point of indecision, at every moment of despair; at every crisis, at every triumph. These words are spoken to inspire and to entreat, to direct and to forgive.

The purpose of this book is threefold:
    To trace with you the paths where Jesus walked.
    To take another long and careful look at the life He lived.
    To ponder the example which He left for us.

All of this is involved if you are to take Him at His word and honor His command, "Follow Me."

Why do I call this the Incredible Command?

It is incredible because of the One who gave it.

What was Jesus doing here, anyway? Why did He have this encounter with these men by Galilee? Why does He have an encounter with you? Who is this Jesus?

The answers to these questions go beyond your wildest flights of imagination. Only divine revelation and the historical fact of Jesus' presence here on this earth can make you believe that the divine Son of God actually came. His very presence was itself incredible.

Why was He here?—

"God so loved the world, that He gave His only begotten Son." He came:

> That He might show you the way to a better, happier life.
> That His blood might erase the record of your sins.
> That His resurrection might give you the assurance of heaven.
> That His mediation might see you through the final judgment.
> That when He comes again you may share in His kingdom.

It is this incredible Jesus who gives to us the Incredible Command, "Follow Me."

When we think of great leaders, our minds go back over the historical record. We find them in the fields of science, discovery, military campaigns, the political arena, and in great religious movements. They stand out. Their records brighten the pages of history both sacred and secular. They tell us a great deal. We learn much from the study of their lives.

Think of men like Alexander and Napoleon—men of tremendous valor and personal magnetism.

Long after Napoleon's death someone asked one of his former soldiers, "Was Napoleon really so great? Why did people follow him so willingly?"

He replied, "If he had commanded us to go to the moon, we would have set out, convinced that he would find a way to get us there."

8 INCREDIBLE COMMAND

Napoleon! There was a man. A great magnetic personality. When he escaped from his first exile in the Mediterranean, he started his march back into France again. History records that the armies sent out to capture him fell in line behind him and joyfully joined his triumphant return!

There have been other great leaders, some good, some bad, who had that kind of personal magnetism. People followed them with blind commitment.

Just outside the city of Yokohama, Japan, on a hill overlooking Tokyo Bay, is a very unusual building. It is octagonal in structure and looks like a temple. The day I visited it there were no crowds around. The old caretaker came out and took me inside.

Curtains were drawn across what seemed to be the center of attraction. At my request he drew back these curtains, and there stood, a little larger than life-size, statues of eight great world leaders: Buddha, Confucius, several others. And among them was a statue of Jesus.

The temple is called the Hall of the Eight, *Hasseiden,* the Hall of the Eight Great Leaders. And Jesus was one of them! In a way it made me happy to see Jesus recognized as a great leader, even by people who do not believe in Him as the Saviour. And yet, it made me sad to think that they considered Him as being merely one among the other seven.

The Jesus who says, "Follow Me," who dares give this Incredible Command, transcends in authority, in power, in magnetism all other great men who have ever lived.

Why? Because He is the Son of God.

But is that all? No. He is also the Son of man. And His appearance on this earth changed the whole course of human history.

Wherever we look in the story of Jesus, we find Him in the center of the picture. He is the chief actor on the stage at every point in the whole drama.

We look at heaven, and there He is, the member of the Godhead chosen to supervise the creation of the universe. (See Colossians 1:13-16; Ephesians 3:9.) Then we see the great conflict begin in heaven itself. Again it is Jesus who commands the armies of heaven, who vanquishes, then banishes Satan and his angels.

And when He comes to this earth, every time he appears on the sacred page, the narrative focuses on Him. See Him as a twelve-year-old boy attending His first Passover. Where do we find Him? Sitting with the teachers and scholars and great leaders of the Jewish nation, asking them questions and answering theirs.

In each of His activities throughout the story, Jesus is the leader. He never does any of the things we expect from ordinary, famous men. Yet somehow He is always at the center:

> Raising Lazarus from the tomb.
> Riding triumphantly into Jerusalem.
> Suffering through the ignominy of His trial.
> Hanging finally on the center cross.

Wherever He is, all eyes are fixed on Him.

After the resurrection, when He ascends to heaven again, we hear that tremendous paean of praise by the angels who accompany Him to the gates of the heavenly city: "Lift up your heads, O ye gates; and be ye lift up, ye everlasting doors; and the King of glory shall come in."

Then sounds the challenge from the holy sentries within: "Who is this King of glory?" And the answer is given: "The Lord of hosts, he is the King of glory." Psalm 24:7-10. See *The Desire of Ages*, p. 833. He continues to hold center stage.

And then, in that glorious day when He keeps His promise to return to this earth again, He Himself as King of kings and Lord of lords will lead forth the hosts of heaven. The vast, bright shining of the glorified sky will draw the attention of the whole world on Jesus as He comes again.

It is this incomparable Leader who says, "Follow Me." It is the Incredible Command because it comes from an incredible Commander.

It is also incredible because Jesus—
> Includes human beings, you and me, in His command,
> Guarantees your success if you respond by following, and
> Promises an incredible reward if you stay with Him till the end.

10 INCREDIBLE COMMAND

Even now, my friend, as you read these lines, do you feel yourself drawn to the Christ of the cross? Do you sense a desire to respond, when He says, "Follow Me."

Do not turn away. Do not say, "How could I possibly follow Him?" Remember that when this incredible Leader gives the command, He also passes on to you the extraordinary ability you need to follow. The act of responding automatically connects you with the power that makes obedience possible.

I invite you to turn these pages with me as we trace the paths where Jesus walked. But first, will you join me now in prayer?

Heavenly Father, we do not know all that it will mean to follow You. We are amazed at the concept. We are intrigued with the challenge. We are disturbed with what may be involved. But we want to know why You have said to us, to each one, "Follow Me." O Lord, we pray that the Christ of the cross with that magnetic drawing power, may lead us to the point where we walk after Him who is the Way, until we have an abundant entrance into His kingdom. For we ask it in the name of Jesus. Amen.

The Path of Simplicity

"Foxes have holes, and birds of the air have nests; but the Son of man hath not where to lay his head." Luke 9:58.

"Jesus shunned display. During all the years of His stay in Nazareth, He made no exhibition of His miraculous power. He sought no high position and assumed no titles. His quiet and simple life . . . [teaches] an important lesson. . . . Jesus is our example."—*The Desire of Ages,* p. 74.

Chapter 2
Shoes, Wheels, or Wings?

Most of us have subscribed to the principle that Jesus is our Saviour. We have accepted Him in His role as Creator and Redeemer. We are looking for His return as Coming King. But have we really come to grips with our response to His Incredible Command, "Follow Me"?

As we look at the life of Jesus, always we must remember that He is Lord of all, Creator of the universe, Possessor of total divine authority, and that to know Him is life eternal. But He is revealed on this earth as a man. What kind of man? How did this supreme Deity demonstrate the life of a human being?

After all, we cannot hope to follow Him in His divine nature. When He said, "Follow Me," He called for us to pattern our lives on His earthly experience.

This human life of Jesus must be the focus of our attention.

In these pages we want to take time to trace the paths where Jesus walked. Our concern, of course, is not with literal geographical locations, but with the lifestyle—His manner, His method, His attitude. Because, if we are to follow Him, these are the paths we will need to cover.

There will be seven of them before we are finished.

As we begin our study of the paths where Jesus walked, the first will be the Path of Simplicity. It is divided into two chapters: "Shoes, Wheels, or Wings?" and "Winsome Magnetism."

This first path introduces us to Jesus' personal lifestyle. In total contrast to what the world expects of its great men, Jesus lived a life of utter simplicity. He neither sought nor needed any material symbols of success.

Jesus made this plain in a number of ways, but on one occasion He enunciated it very distinctly. A man who had been watching Jesus and His disciples decided he could identify with them. He wanted to join the group. So he presented himself. Jesus had called the other disciples. This man volunteered.

At first glance we might praise him for his initiative. He didn't wait to be asked. He was one of those who said, "Here I am; send me." But on closer examination of the story, we find he doesn't deserve that kind of commendation.

Who was this man? Judas.[1]

He presented a fine appearance. He looked like a businessman. He seemed to have a background of both experience and erudition, qualities the other disciples lacked. Most of them were from common pursuits—fishermen, tax collectors, and so on. Not Judas. He was a cut above the others. The disciples felt that a man like him could bring them all a little prestige. Perhaps they even encouraged him to come to Jesus.

Judas said, "Master, I will follow thee withersoever thou goest."

Now notice, Jesus didn't say to him, "Follow Me." He said to Jesus, "I will follow thee."

Jesus' answer gave on that occasion reveals His character. "Foxes have holes, and the birds of the air have nests; but the Son of man hath not where to lay His head." Matthew 8:19, 20. He set before Judas a principle of His kingdom, a principle which Judas did not understand and which he never accepted.

Despite all this, Jesus admitted Judas to the ranks of the Twelve. He was ordained along with the others. He went on the missionary journeys. He carried a responsible position as treasurer of the group. He gave every appearance of being an outstanding disciple.

Yet Judas never felt comfortable in this role of simplicity. He didn't like the idea that the Son of man had not where to lay His head. His unwillingness to accept Jesus' philosophy led to his inevitable disaster.

Jesus never swerved from the path He had outlined. His

style of living during His entire earthly experience was characterized by this unique simplicity.

How Jesus Rated Material Things

Remember the Sermon on the Mount?

Jesus talked about the birds. He talked about the flowers. He said that Solomon in all his glory couldn't compare with them in beauty. And then He made the remarkable statement: "Take no thought, saying, What shall we eat? or, What shall we drink? or, Wherewithal shall we be clothed? . . . Your heavenly Father knoweth that ye have need of all these things."

Finally He put it all in perspective: "But seek ye first the kingdom of God, and his righteousness; and all these things shall be added unto you." Matthew 6:31-33.

We find His philosophy of simplicity in the instructions He gave His disciples when He sent them on their first ministerial assignment. They were to travel light. Their luggage included no extra items of clothing or equipment. They were to accept what people gave them and stay where they were invited.

Did you ever stop to consider that, aside from the time when Jesus as a tiny baby went to Egypt in His mother's arms, there is no record of His riding on anything until He made His triumphal entry into Jerusalem near the close of His life? And then it was on a borrowed burro. He had no animal of His own.

His was a simple life. He walked. As a result, Jesus never traveled very far. During His entire ministry He never visited any point farther than about one hundred miles from His headquarters in Galilee. And the story of the Good Samaritan gives us some idea of how rough and dangerous those roads could be.

I suppose Jesus could have had a chariot or a horse or at least a burro. But He walked—which is why this chapter is entitled "Shoes, Wheels, or Wings?" Jesus could have had His choice.

You remember the time the devil took Him up to a pinnacle of the temple? "Cast thyself down," Satan said, "for it is written, He shall give his angels charge concerning thee: and in their hands they shall bear thee up, lest at any time thou dash thy foot against a stone." Matthew 4:6.

"There are wings for you," said the tempter. "Go ahead and jump." But Jesus spurned the wings. He wouldn't call on His divine power to satisfy the devil.

Notice how all the habits of Jesus' life emphasized simplicity:
　　His spiritual exercises,
　　His social activities,
　　His clothing, food, and housing, and
　　His teaching methods.

All of these offered a sharp contrast to the religious leaders who spurned Him.

He mingled with the common people—not only with those who were poor, but also with those who were known to be sinners. This the Jewish leaders couldn't tolerate. "Why," they cried, "this man eats with publicans and sinners." Contrast this with Jesus' statement: "I came not to call the righteous, but sinners to repentance." Mark 2:17.

When He preached or taught, people could understand Him. Not always could this be said of the religious leaders of the day. They loved to couch their scholarly discussions concerning the law in terms which showed their erudition. But Jesus, the record says, "taught them as one having authority, and not as the scribes"—"and the common people heard him gladly." Matthew 7:29; Mark 12:37. They could understand what He said. It was clear and simple.

In all His daily living, Jesus demonstrated a comfortable thriftiness. And yet His very simplicity carried a degree of distinction. He could enter the impoverished dwellings of the poor or the palaces of the wealthy without embarrassment to either them or Him.

Nothing in Jesus' lifestyle resembled a hippie-type culture. His priorities were in perfect adjustment. His simplicity included no shoddiness, no attempt to appear low-class or cheap. Neither did He show any pride of appearance or ostentation.

He made the simple life winsome and attractive.

Our Path of Simplicity

What will our lives be like if we follow Jesus in the path of simplicity?

To begin with, we must recognize that genuine simplicity is basically a matter of mental attitude.

This is where we often fail. We think that simplicity depends on the things we own—the house we live in, the type of clothes we wear, the car we drive. But the really important factor is our attitude toward these things.

We live in a world filled with contrived simplicity. We might call these fabulous fads. Having spent most of my working life overseas, I found it fascinating to come back to the United States and see some of the currently popular items. As an example, it amused me to see the denim fabric was prefaded before being made into new garments!

Now please do not misunderstand me. I think wearing denim jeans is just fine for casual occasions. But you'll have to admit that faded denim does not always stand for simplicity in dress, especially when sewn into designer jeans!

The characteristic that is required when Christ says, "Follow Me in the Path of Simplicity," is a proper mental attitude—not only about the things we own, but also about the way we use them. Our attitude will result from a deliberate calculation based on ultimate worth.

Where is our sense of values? This is what determines real simplicity. It is based on what we need, not on what we want.

The psalmist wrote, "The Lord is my shepherd; I shall not want." Psalm 23:1. Obviously he expressed the idea that he could trust God for all his necessities. Perhaps the text could be paraphrased to read, "I shall not want anything I don't really need." Most of us get into trouble because of the things we want.

Some time ago when I was in the Far Eastern Division office in Singapore, one of our departmental directors made a trip to Korea. On her return she came to my office and presented me with a little gift.

I opened the box and found a small but beautiful piece of granite, highly polished—just a little stone. It had a hollowed-out place on one side that fit my thumb perfectly as I held the stone in the palm of my hand.

A slip of paper that came along with the gift informed me

that this was a worry stone. The idea was to sit at the desk in the midst of my most difficult problems, hold that stone in my hand, and rub gently with my thumb in that indentation. This was supposed to ease my mind. Perhaps such activity could be called fingertip transcendental meditation!

Actually, the most valuable feature of this whimsical little gift was a single sentence near the end of the instruction. This I have not forgotten. "Happiness and tranquility will come to those who want only what they have."

Now *there* is a priceless gem of oriental wisdom! "Happiness and tranquility will come to those who want only what they have." It sounds very much like the apostle Paul. "I have learned, in whatsoever state I am, therewith to be content." Philippians 4:11.

This is the mental attitude that leads us to follow in the simple path where Jesus walked. It is based on what we need and not on what we want.

The Tyranny of Material Possessions

We live in a world today where always wanting more and better things has become a global obsession. It affects whole nations as well as individuals. The result: a worldwide passion for overspending.

Both people and nations are saying: "Others have these things. I want them too. And I want them *now!*"

So they mortgage their futures, then spend the rest of their lives struggling to pay off their obligations. This is one of today's most common forms of mental anguish.

God wants to spare us from this kind of anxiety.

Now I don't mean to imply that it is necessarily wrong to feel a need of some things that we do not have. Neither is it always sinful to have nice things. It isn't by definition wrong to travel first class. Riding on wheels instead of walking is a good idea, or on wings if that is what will get us there to do our work faster and better.

The question of "Shoes, Wheels, or Wings?" is one of attitude toward those things. We should never be held hostage to tyranny of material possessions. We must develop a sense of values that lets the spirit of Jesus control our desires. The psalmist says, "If riches increase, set not your heart upon them." Psalm 62:10.

For illustration, watch a group of children playing.

Some are having a great time with nothing but a crude set of blocks made up of scraps of wood brought home by the carpenter father. And right beside them you may see other children who are testy, quarrelsome, and throwing tantrums while they try to decide who will run the controls of the electric train.

Carry the point a little farther, and you will find doctors who are perfectly happy with Fords and other doctors who are disgruntled with their Lincoln Continental because they would rather have a Rolls Royce.

Please, I don't want to leave any impression that it isn't good to have nice things, or that to have them is synonymous with denying the Lord. Not so. Jesus Himself liked nice things. He accepted the hospitality of Zacchaeus in his beautiful home. He went to Simon's feast. He didn't hesitate to associate with those of wealth and prominence. But He didn't need those things to make Him happy. His mental attitude registered them as unimportant. There were other things that required His attention.

Let me tell you of two visits I made during the early days of my ministry.

On one occasion I stepped into the home of an elderly couple. All their friends knew that they were well off. And yet they lived in a home which most of us would consider filthy. It was cluttered with the accumulation of years. The rugs were threadbare. Every piece of furniture needed to be refinished or reupholstered. They were wealthy, but they lived among junk. And they had a reputation of being misers.

Later I stepped into another home, the home of a Black woman who had been widowed early in life. She had reared her children alone, with hardly any steady income, and yet an atmosphere of genuine Christianity permeated her house.

Isolated, far out in the country, they lived in a little one-room house—bedroom, living room, kitchen all in one. And yet that room was absolutely spotless. You could have eaten off the floor. They lived below the poverty level. But there was happiness in that home.

How is it with you? What kind of simple life do you live?

To lay down this book and say, "From now on I'm going to show that I'm really living simply," would be to completely miss the point. Because it is the mental attitude that is important.

How do you feel about *things*? Are you tied to them? Can you make do with only the barest essentials and still maintain your dignity? Can you live in an expensive condominium, surrounded with luxury, without feeling smug?

Many people today are like Judas. They are just not comfortable with this simplicity concept. They say, "The church would attract more people if only it had a little more class."

Certainly we all are interested in making the Christian life appear in the most favorable light. Do we need more-expensive church buildings? Or a larger percentage of financially successful members? What can we do to exert before the world the greatest possible drawing power?

Our next chapter looks at this idea. It is entitled "Winsome Magnetism."

And now, will you join me in a moment of prayer?

Heavenly Father, Thank You for sending your Son Jesus, not as a great and powerful ruler, but as One who lived a life of beautiful simplicity. Thank You for giving us this wonderful Saviour who was loved by the children, by the sick and troubled, by the wealthy and the poor, by the sinner and the saint. Give us, Lord, the kind of genuinely humble spirit that will make it possible for us to follow Jesus in this Path of Simplicity. For we ask it in His name. Amen.

---

1. *The Desire of Ages,* pp. 293-295.

Chapter 3
Winsome Magnetism

In our previous chapter we noticed how difficult it is for people to grasp the significance of the simplicity which characterized the life of Jesus. The human heart clamors for display. Our senses, bombarded daily by media extravaganzas of brilliant color and movement, have come to expect this kind of excitement.

We should not be surprised, then, that many people think the church needs to adopt some of these ideas to get its message across. Indeed, many of the world's religions feature magnificent pageants, gilded temples, and massed multitudes gathered in pilgrimages to famous shrines.

What did Jesus say about capturing the attention of the world? "And I, if I be lifted up from the earth, will draw all men unto me. This he said, signifying what death he should die." John 12:32, 33. He was talking about the cross. Could there be a more stunning example of simplicity than those crossed beams of rough-hewn wood? Yet the figure of Jesus hanging on that cross has commanded the attention of the whole world.

While serving as a missionary in Japan, I became acquainted with Fujimori, a young man who lived in Nagano prefecture, about a hundred miles northwest of Tokyo. His is a remarkable story.

During the days just after the end of World War II, the Japanese people found themselves in desperate circumstances. Fujimori was a typical example. He decided he had nothing left to live for. He would follow the honorable Japanese tradition, commit suicide, and end it all.

Fujimori used his imagination. He chose an unusual method to commit suicide. Back of his home a high-tension line led from the hydroelectric plant in the mountains to the city's industrial area. He knew those wires were charged with a tremendous voltage of electricity. He concluded that he could climb one of those great steel towers, seize a wire, and end everything in a blinding flash.

One night, with the stars shining with unusual brilliance, Fujimori set out to accomplish his plan. Finding a tower not far from his home, he stood at the foot, ready to start his climb. Looking up, he noticed the outline of the tower silhouetted against the sky. It gripped his attention. He almost gasped. "The cross!"

Fujimori, though not a Christian, had heard about the cross. He thought to himself, "That's something I've never tried." He postponed his suicide plan. He asked among his friends if anyone knew about the cross and Jesus Christ.

Finally someone showed him an old book about the Bible. Fujimori borrowed it, took it home, and started to read. It was a Japanese translation of Uriah Smith's book *Daniel and Revelation.*

Fujimori, an intelligent and well-educated fellow, read that book with increasing fascination. He began to think, "I must give this book back to my friend," and so he did an incredible thing. He sat down with note paper and pen and copied the whole book by hand!

In the process he came to the flyleaf, which gave the address of the publishers, the Japan Publishing House of Seventh-day Adventists. He wrote a letter to the publishers and asked if he could purchase more literature.

This letter reached our headquarters in Tokyo. The problem was that the publishing house had been closed and the stocks of books long since destroyed during the war. However, one of the workers sent a set of Japanese Voice of Prophecy Bible Correspondence lessons to Fujimori.

With keen interest he started studying. Convinced he had

found the truth, he wrote again, requesting a visit from a pastor. When a worker finally got to Fujimori, he found him ready for baptism. I met Fujimori several years later in the Nagano church, where he served as one of the lay leaders.

Fujimori had discovered the winsome magnetism, which is the drawing power of the cross. He had exchanged his despair and his plans for suicide for obedience to the Incredible Command, "Follow Me."

Dignity in Simplicity

The life of true simplicity is a life of dignity. It is a life of charm. As exemplified in the experience of Jesus, it is never one of crudeness. Some people equate simplicity with slovenliness. That is not at all the way Christ considered it.

Take the question of our speech. It is important that we should enunciate clearly and correctly in our daily conversation. I am distressed when I hear people use slovenly speech. Careless use of words, poor grammar, repeated slang expressions, loud, boisterous voices—these give the impression that the individual doesn't care what he sounds like.

Jesus spoke clearly and correctly. He spoke tenderly. Ellen White describes his speech this way: "He was never rude, never needlessly spoke a severe word, never gave needless pain to a sensitive soul. He did not censure human weakness. He fearlessly denounced hypocrisy, unbelief, and iniquity, but tears were in His voice as He uttered His scathing rebukes."[1]

When Jesus spoke, even children listened. Gentleness mingled with authority reached the hearts of all who heard Him.

I have a friend in Japan, whom I first met more than fifty years ago. A brilliant young man, he was principal of our Adventist girls' school in Tokyo. As the years passed he has developed into a skillful administrator, an excellent teacher, a genuine scholar. He came from an important family. In Japan there is a quiet, but carefully observed, sense of social status.

I became very well-acquainted with him through the years. He is one of our very finest Japanese workers. He served at various times as president of our college, editor of our publishing house, and speaker of the Voice of Prophecy radio broadcast in Japan.

He has written more books than any other of our Japanese leaders, and these books are loved and widely read. A number of years ago, in recognition of his major contributions to the church, Andrews University awarded him an honorary doctor's degree.

The man is Dr. Toshio Yamagata. He is a giant among men. And yet, when he speaks everyone listens. Strangely enough, despite his erudition or perhaps because of it, he speaks a simple language. I've wondered just what it is about him that makes him different from so many other speakers, some of whom I have a hard time following.

But, when I listen to Dr. Yamagata, I can understand. His message is clear, logical, beautiful, simple. When he speaks, every person, no matter what his social status, is intrigued by his words; and what he writes they read. And they can understand. He has that priceless quality of simplicity, without in any way sacrificing the dignity and charm that go with genuine culture.

Not only Jesus' life, but also His teachings were characterized by simplicity. His words, "For God so loved the world, that he gave his only begotten Son, that whosoever believeth in him should not perish, but have everlasting life" (John 3:16), are simplicity itself. This simplicity of doctrine is one of the things that distinguishes Christianity from all other great world religions. It is expressed in the words of Paul: "Believe on the Lord Jesus Christ, and thou shalt be saved." Acts 16:31.

We spent most of our lives working for the church in the Far East. We discovered that the very simplicity of the gospel is one of the major problems in working for the people of the Orient. From infancy they are taught to regard religion as some kind of philosophical concept shrouded in mysteries. They find it difficult to grasp that salvation is possible through simply believing in one Man, Jesus Christ.

The apostle Paul understood this problem. He wrote: "The Jews require a sign, and the Greeks seek after wisdom: But we preach Christ crucified, unto the Jews a stumblingblock, and unto the Greeks foolishness." And then he added, "I determined not to know any thing among you, save Jesus Christ, and him crucified." 1 Corinthians 1:22, 23; 2:2.

By His life, by His doctrine, and by the amazing circumstances of His death, Jesus reveals the secret of His winsome, magnetic power. He knows that if you will follow Him in the Path of Simplicity, your life will reflect a measure of that same attraction.

Simple Christian Living Is a Powerful Witness

Not long before the outbreak of World War II, while serving our church in Manila, I had a remarkable experience which illustrates the powerful witness of simple, sincere Christian lives.

One day a stranger came to my home.

He held in his hand a letter from the president of our mission in the southern Philippines. The letter, addressed to me, introduced this man, Douglas Coles, and requested that I study the Bible with him. I read the letter, welcomed him to my home, and listened to an amazing story.

Coles, an Australian, left his country while still a young man, and made his way to the islands of the South Pacific. There he found employment on a coconut plantation. Ambitious and willing to work, Coles soon became manager of the plantation. As a bachelor with money to spend, he found amusement in smoking, drinking and partying. He was very much a man of the world.

The workers on the plantation were local black men from the island villages. Most of them were rather rough characters. But two or three were different. When they got their pay, instead of getting drunk, they went home. He never saw them smoke. They were never in any kind of trouble. They kept regular work hours. They were dependable.

However, he noticed one strange thing about them. They would not work on Saturday.

Intrigued with these boys, Coles questioned some of the villagers about them. The reply was: "They are Christians. They go to the Seventh-day Adventist Mission."

"Well," he thought, "they don't smoke, they don't drink, they don't hang around gambling with the other fellows. But what do they do for fun?" He shook his head and then added: "There's one thing sure. If I ever should become a Christian, I wouldn't be a Seventh-day Adventist!"

As the years passed, Coles moved through the islands, always in the coconut business. Finally he came to the Philippines. Here he found a good job as manager of a coconut desiccating plant where copra was processed for export. Among the young Filipinos working for him was a chap named Elpidio. Coles said to himself, "Now here is a fine worker. I can depend on him." And then he discovered that Elpidio was a Seventh-day Adventist who had arranged to have every Saturday off!

About this time, the plant foreman left rather suddenly. Coles had to find a new foreman. He chose Elpidio to replace him. He called Elpidio into his office.

"Elpidio, I'd like you to take over as plant foreman. Your salary will be just about double what you are making now. There's just one thing though, Elpidio. You'll have to forget about this Saturday business."

Elpidio looked at him soberly for a moment. Then he smiled slowly and said, "Well, if you don't mind, then, I'd rather keep my present job. You see, I can't work on Saturday. That's my Sabbath, and I go to church that day."

After Elpidio had left his office, Coles shook his head in amazement. "Here I offer him a big promotion with almost twice the pay, and he turns it down because he won't work on Saturday! How foolish can you get? There's one thing sure. If I ever became a Christian, I wouldn't be a Seventh-day Adventist."

Some time later, Coles visited the city of Manila. Walking down the street, he noticed two young ladies approaching. They were nice-looking girls. The girls stepped up to him and politely asked him if he would care to buy one of the magazines they were selling. He wasn't especially attracted to the magazine, but he liked the appearance of the girls, so he bought it. He took it home. He read it. And he discovered it was a Seventh-day Adventist magazine.

"And I thought they were such fine-looking girls," he said to himself. "Does everyone who looks good to me have to turn out to be an Adventist? There's one thing sure. If I ever became a Christian, I would not be a Seventh-day Adventist."

Finally he decided he should stop handling coconuts and do something else with his life. He took the money he had saved, moved to the city of Iloilo, and set himself up in a small merchandising business. The store didn't do well at all. He knew a lot about coconuts, but not about running a merchandising business. He closed his shop, sold off his remaining stock to pay his bills, and sat down in his home to face the future. He had no job. He had no friends. He had no family. And he had no God.

Suddenly he realized that he needed help desperately. The first thing that came to his mind jolted him. "You need the Seventh-day Adventist kind of God."

"Oh, no!" He clenched his fist and stalked up and down in his small room. "I will not be an Adventist! I will *not* be an Adventist! I will NOT be an Adventist!" And then he went to the telephone and called the Adventist mission! He asked to talk to the pastor.

The mission president picked up the phone and heard in amazement an agitated voice saying, "Please come and see me. I want to be a Seventh-day Adventist!"

Completely humbled and now eager for truth, Coles began studying with the mission president, an American missionary. After a few weeks he succeeded in finding a job in Manila and asked the mission president to introduce him to an Adventist minister in that city, and this is how I became acquainted with Douglas Coles.

Confined to an internment camp when the Japanese army occupied Manila, Coles continued studying with an Adventist pastor, who was also a prisoner there. This pastor baptized Coles in the camp, and after the war he returned to Australia.

I heard nothing more of him for many years. Then, just before I left the Far East to return to America to retire, I received a letter from Douglas Coles.

28 INCREDIBLE COMMAND

"I found your address. I want you to know that I am still a Seventh-day Adventist. I am retired and live here in Brisbane."

What led Douglas Coles, against his will, to find his Saviour? The quiet, consistent witness of several children of God who were following Jesus in the Path of Simplicity.

My friend, how is it with you?

Jesus says, "Follow Me."

Heavenly Father, we recognize that there is in us no good thing, that even our basic attitudes have not been shaped to grasp what it means to live the kind of simple life that Jesus lived. But we thank You for that life. For its dignity, its charm, its culture, and its power. We thank You for calling us, for giving us the privilege of walking where Jesus walked. We pray that we may follow with dignity, with grace, with sincerity. For we ask it in Jesus' name. Amen.

---

1. *The Desire of Ages,* p. 353.

The Path of Supplication

"In the morning, rising up a great while before day, he went out, and departed into a solitary place, and there prayed." Mark 1:35.

"In Christ the cry of humanity reached the Father of infinite pity. As a man He supplicated the throne of God till His humanity was charged with a heavenly current that should connect humanity with divinity. Through continual communion He received life from God, that He might impart life to the world. His experience is to be ours."—*The Desire of Ages,* p. 363.

Chapter 4
"Give Us This Day . . ."

As Jesus began His ministry on this earth, He eagerly searched the faces of those who listened to Him, looking for some flicker of interest, some evidence of conviction. To those who responded He gave the simple but profound invitation: "Follow Me." This is the Incredible Command.

It is still the same today. Have you heard this voice? Have you felt yourself drawn to follow Him? Then join me as we continue to discover the paths where He walked, when He led His disciples through the towns and villages of Palestine. It is in these paths that we may follow Him and pattern our lives on His example.

We have already considered the Path of Simplicity. Now we will focus on path number two: the Path of Supplication. This will be covered in three chapters, the first entitled, "Give Us This Day. . . ."

Soon after responding to Jesus' call, "Follow Me," the disciples began to notice how often He communed with His Father in heaven. They had never seen anything like it. Jesus made this an important feature of His daily life and work. He began His days with private prayer. He prayed at every time of crisis. He prayed before every important decision, and the disciples came to realize that this unbroken contact with the heavenly Father provided the source of His power.

We should not be surprised, therefore, to hear them say to Jesus, "Lord, teach us to pray."

Do you feel that way too? Would you like to improve your connection with heaven? Do you want to be sure you can always get through to God with your requests? Whether we realize it or not, this is a universal concern.

I discovered this a number of years ago when the school where we were teaching in Japan scheduled a picnic. The whole student body and faculty took an all-day trip to see a famous Buddhist shrine, more than a thousand years old.

Built on the very top of a mountain, it made a spectacular impression. Huge pillars, each made from the trunk of a large tree, supported the temple that clung, as it were, to the peak. A kind of veranda extended from the entrance all the way around the shrine, making a fine observation walkway for both sightseers like ourselves, and worshipers.

As I stood near the entrance, my attention focused on a little old Japanese woman. Bent from long years of toil, probably in the rice fields, she was making her way slowly around the building and returned to the main entrance. There she paused and faced the temple. Clapping her hands together in a precise and ceremonious fashion, she bowed deeply and prayed. Then I noticed that from a little packet held in her hand she took one grain of rice and deposited it in a small receptacle fastened to one of the pillars.

Having completed her brief prayer, she started around the temple veranda again. She didn't walk very fast. Soon she disappeared from my sight, only to reappear moments later, having passed behind the temple, and now heading once more toward the entrance. There she paused, facing the shrine itself, clapped her hands together ceremoniously, bowed in an attitude of prayer, then took from the little packet another grain of rice and placed it in the receptacle on the pillar. Then she started off again.

I don't know how many circuits she made around the temple. But her obvious sincerity and earnestness intrigued me, so I asked one of our Japanese teachers to explain the meaning of her actions.

He replied, "No doubt she has some problem and is seeking divine help in solving it. She is probably staying in one of these houses down just below the shrine and will come here each day for a whole month. Every morning she will make the circuit of the shrine *one hundred* times, praying each time she faces the temple entrance. She counts the grains of rice before she gets to the temple, and when the grains have all been deposited she knows she has finished for that day."

This experience did something to me. Of course, I admired the woman's piety and earnestness. But in addition to my admiration I also felt a great sorrow. She did not know that there is an easier yet more effective way of finding an answer to her prayers.

If only she could have known the simplicity and satisfaction of following Jesus in the Path of Supplication!

Private Prayer—Public Power

Jesus lived a life in which prayer became the central feature.

If we study His experience we find that He began His lifework with a public act of prayer. When John the Baptist administered the rite of baptism to Jesus at the Jordan River, the latter paused on the bank as He came up out of the water. The record says, "that Jesus also being baptized, and praying, the heaven was opened, and the Holy Ghost descended in a bodily shape like a dove upon him, and a voice came from heaven, which said, Thou art my beloved Son; in thee I am well pleased." Luke 3:21, 22.

And then, about three and a half years later, His ministry ended with a tragedy, which turned out to be a triumph, when He died upon the cross. His last words were another prayer: "Father, into thy hands I commend my spirit." Luke 23:46.

Between these two events, all through His life's experiences, Jesus seemed eager to pray. He walked daily in this Path of Supplication. But beside public prayers, he also had a regular system of private devotions. One record, from the early days of His ministry, says: "In the morning, rising up a great while before day, he went out, and departed into a solitary place, and there prayed." Mark 1:35. From this and other references we get a picture of regular and earnest sessions of secret prayer.

34 INCREDIBLE COMMAND

Notice also the following occasions when Jesus engaged in urgent private prayer for specific situations:

1. Immediately after His baptism, with the awesome responsibility of His earthly mission bearing upon Him, Jesus went into the wilderness and spent forty days in devotion. See Matthew 4:1-11.

2. Just before ordaining the twelve disciples, Jesus spent the entire night in prayer. See Luke 6:12-16.

3. Sometime later, after Jesus had miraculously fed the multitude and there had been an attempt to make Him a king, the record says, "He departed again into a mountain himself alone." John 6:15.

We have this inspired description of what these sessions of prayer did for Jesus: "No other life was ever so crowded with labor and responsibility as was that of Jesus; yet how often He was found in prayer!

"As one with us, a sharer in our needs and weaknesses, He was wholly dependent upon God, and in the secret place of prayer He sought divine strength, that He might go forth braced for duty and trial. In a world of sin Jesus endured struggles and torture of soul. In communion with God He could unburden the sorrows that were crushing Him. Here He found comfort and joy."[1]

One time on a visit to New York City I went into the beautiful Riverside Church. It is a magnificent edifice. The tower of that church rises more than thirty stories and contains the offices for a very busy spiritual practice. The main nave is a marvelous triumph of architecture, seating some three thousand. Downstairs is an overflow hall, which can hold almost as many more who can, by electronic means, be present at the services in the main sanctuary. However, the object that impressed me most about that beautiful church was located in a small room, a tiny chapel, on the far side of the narthex. There on the wall hangs the original oil masterpiece of Hoffman's "Christ Praying in Gethsemane."

It is impossible to stand there and look at that picture without being moved.

Some of the reproductions of this painting have been

lightened considerably, showing details of the folds of His clothing and other features. But the original is dark and somber. After all, Jesus offered that prayer at night in the garden.

The painting captures Him in the act of communion with His Father. That night His soul cried out for this intimate consultation with His source of wisdom, power, and encouragement.

Jesus prayed, "O my Father, if it be possible, let this cup pass from me: nevertheless not as I will, but as thou wilt." Matthew 26:39.

At that moment the salvation of all the world trembled on the lips of the kneeling Christ. Talking with His Father offered the only possible source of the strength He needed. This was the sublime moment of supplication. Not just for Himself, but supplication for all the world, for you, for me.[2]

From that prayer Jesus received enough strength to drink the cup His Father could not take from His hands if the plan were to be fulfilled.

"Lord, Teach Us to Pray"

During His life and ministry Jesus not only prayed Himself; He willingly discussed the subject of prayer with others. He was pleased when the disciples said, "Lord, teach us to pray."

Certainly they had been praying since childhood. They understood much about God. They believed in Him. But something about the way Jesus prayed convinced them that their own prayers were not all that they should be. They wanted to learn to pray as Jesus prayed. In answer to that request, Jesus gave them the Lord's Prayer. It is from this prayer that we get our topic for this chapter; "Give us this day. . . . " Familiar as we are with the Lord's Prayer, it deserves our frequent and thoughtful study. It is perfect in its reverence, complete in its requests, and total in its praise.

Jesus taught that we should be persevering in prayer. He urged us not to give up too quickly. Sometimes we have difficulty in understanding this. But Jesus made it clear. He Himself prayed that way. Is it because God doesn't hear us the first time? Is it because He doesn't want to answer until He first puts us through a bit of grueling effort?

Certainly these cannot be the reasons. No doubt the persevering is for our benefit, though we often wonder why the answers take so long. Jesus makes it clear, however, that there is a certain efficacy in earnest, fervent, persevering prayer.

Not only did Jesus teach His disciples to pray; He also taught them how not to pray. He rebuked hypocrisy in prayer. Remember the story of the Pharisee and the publican who went into the temple for their devotions? See Luke 18:10-13.

He cautioned His disciples to beware of long, repetitious prayers. "When ye pray, use not vain repetitions, as the heathen do.... Your Father knoweth what things ye have need of, before ye ask him." Matthew 6:7, 8.

Each time the disciples heard Jesus pray, they had a fresh opportunity to learn the how, when, and why of effective prayer. Notice the following examples:

They heard Jesus pray at Lazarus's tomb. Then they watched, enthralled, as He turned to the sepulcher and commanded: "Lazarus, come forth." See John 11:41-43.

The disciples were present when some Greeks came by one day with the request, "We would see Jesus." The disciples passed the request on to Jesus. He continued talking to the multitude, but now He spoke especially for the benefit of these strangers. He merged this conversation with an unexpected prayer directed to heaven.

"Father, glorify thy name," He prayed.

With an instantaneous answer God spoke: "I have both glorified it, and will glorify it again." See John 12:20-30.

Some of the crowd thought they heard thunder. Others said that an angel had spoken to Jesus. But the Greeks heard and understood. They had asked to see Jesus, and God Himself had honored their search with this audible voice.

The disciples had seen another example of prayer in action. On the night before His crucifixion, after the Lord's Supper, the disciples heard Jesus' longest recorded prayer. Their hearts were moved because Jesus was praying for them. See John 17.

And so, by direct instruction and by example, Jesus answered the disciples' request, "Lord, teach us to pray."

Listen to these inspired words:

"In Christ the cry of humanity reached the Father of infinite pity. As a man He supplicated the throne of God till His humanity was charged with a heavenly current that should connect humanity with divinity. Through continual communion He received life from God, that He might impart life to the world." Then, this significant sentence: "His experience is to be ours."[3]

Could it be put more succinctly? "His experience is to be ours." The call is clear. Jesus says, "Follow Me in the Path of Supplication."

Heavenly Father, our hearts echo the request of the disciples, "Lord, teach us to pray." We want to follow Jesus in the Path of Supplication. We thank You for giving us in the Scriptures the record of Jesus' life of prayer. We thank You that He loved us enough to include us in His prayers. Give us the wisdom to trace the paths where He walked, and the courage to follow Him there. For we ask it in His name. Amen.

---

1. *The Desire of Ages,* p. 363.
2. *Ibid.,* pp. 686-694.
3. *Ibid.,* p. 363.

Chapter 5
Heaven—Earth: Direct Communication Connection

Our previous chapter introduced the concept that accepting the Incredible Command, "Follow me," will inevitably lead us to trace the steps of Jesus in the Path of Supplication.

Did you find yourself joining the disciples in their request, "Lord, teach us to pray?" Did you wish you could have the same kind of intimate relationship that Jesus had with His heavenly Father? Did you long for a measure of the assurance and power Jesus experienced when He prayed?

I have good news for you. You have access to the very same communication system that Jesus used. Prayer offers you a direct connection between heaven and earth. And Jesus says you can use His name when you find yourself talking to His Father.

No doubt you are familiar with many of the following beautiful quotations about prayer:

"Prayer is the breath of the soul. It is the secret of spiritual power."[1]

"Prayer is the opening of the heart to God as to a friend."[2]

"Prayer is the key in the hand of faith to unlock heaven's storehouse, where are treasured the boundless resources of Omnipotence."[3]

These are inspired definitions of prayer. You have doubtless read over them again and again. But now you must apply them to your personal experience. How will your daily lifestyle be affected when you actually answer the Saviour's call and follow Him in the Path of Supplication?

When you face the same kinds of crisis and trial that Jesus faced, you want to be able to pray as He prayed. You want to follow Him also in the path of daily, private prayer. Make these daily prayer sessions personal and specific. Make a conscious effort to be sincere.

As a small boy, I remember distinctly a period of time early each morning when contact with my dad was off limits. His study remained closed. We were not supposed to knock on the door of his study. He was praying and studying.

How often I passed that room—I can remember it still—and heard his voice on the other side of that door. Occasionally he sounded near to tears. "O God!" "O Lord!" I don't know what he prayed about, but I remember that he found something important to discuss with his heavenly Father every morning.

My father was a Seventh-day Adventist minister, and his prayer life left an indelible impression on me. One time, when I was just entering the ministry myself, he said, "There's a passage in volume five of the *Testimonies* that's very important."

Then he read me this single sentence: "Everyone must now search the Bible for himself upon his knees before God, with the humble, teachable heart of a child, if he would know what the Lord requires of him."[4] He repeated it with emphasis: *"Everyone must now search the Bible for himself upon his knees before God."*

He looked at me and smiled. Then he said simply, "I have read the Bible all the way through *twice on my knees.*"

Now I began to understand a little of what had been going on behind that closed door of his study every morning for so many years. Think of how many people have never read the whole Bible through even once, seated in a comfortable chair! My father had found his comfort, his strength for victory, his power for ministry on his knees before God.

You don't need to be told that you ought to pray. What you need is stimulation to pray as you should, and as often as you should. This stimulation can come from many sources.

One of these is the realization that you can't get by without prayer. Besides your constant need, there will surely come sudden, desperate situations. How thankful we should be that prayer is not limited to either time or place. It is a "hot line," if you please. Always and instantly available, whenever it is needed.

Another stimulation to pray comes, not from a great loss or a threatened disaster, but from a simple desire to get acquainted with God.

I like that approach. We ought to be personal about it. We ought to want to get to know Him better. How could we find a higher-placed Friend?

We feel delighted and perhaps a little flattered when we have the chance to meet personally some important individual whom the world applauds. I remember an experience I had in Japan shortly after the close of World War II.

During the occupation of that country, General Douglas MacArthur was Supreme Commander for the Allied Powers. These initials, SCAP, formed the acronym for the entire occupation command.

General MacArthur and his staff had their offices in the Dai-Ichi Insurance building, one of the few important structures in downtown Tokyo that had survived the bombs. Architecturally imposing, this building stood on a main thoroughfare just across the moat from the ancient outer walls of the castle grounds which surround the emperor's palace. A very appropriate situation for the headquarters of the occupying powers! General MacArthur's office was located at the front corner of the sixth floor.

I decided I would like to meet the general. My wife had written a book about our experience as internees in a prison camp in the Philippines under the Japanese during the war. Since mention of General MacArthur appeared in her book, I thought that presenting him a copy would offer a good opportunity to meet him.

One day I spoke to the captain who was my regular contact with the section of the army dealing with missionary activities. I told him of my wish to meet General MacArthur.

He said, "Give me a little time to work on it. The General is interested in the work of missionaries, and I think I can arrange an interview through regular channels." (Anyone who has had anything to do with the military knows the importance as well as the frustrations of working through channels!)

Several weeks later the captain informed me, "It's all worked out. General MacArthur will see you. Call Colonel Wheeler. He'll give you an appointment."

I called Colonel Wheeler, the general's aide. Despite their sometimes devious nature, channels can be very effective. The colonel, an affable man, said, "The general will see you in his office on Monday evening, at six o'clock."

Excited at the prospect, you may be sure I kept that appointment on time! Dressed in a new suit and not a little nervous, I entered the Dai-Ichi building. Military police, in snappy uniforms, stood guard at the entrance, at the elevators, and on every floor. But they did not delay me. After all, I had an appointment!

Colonel Wheeler greeted me warmly. "The ambassador is talking to the general right now," he said, "but he'll be out in a minute."

Soon the ambassador accompanied by a two-star general came out of MacArthur's office. The colonel went inside. In just a few moments he came out again.

"The general will see you now."

I stepped through the door into the large, luxurious office. With a warm smile, General MacArthur took several long strides across the thick carpet with his hand stretched out to greet me. I will always remember this as one of the most exciting moments of my life.

On each shoulder of his uniform, arranged around a blood-red ruby, were the five silver stars of his rank. Perhaps the most brilliant strategist America ever produced, General MacArthur had led the triumphal conquest of the Pacific theater that had now culminated in the occupation of Japan. The Emperor of Japan had come humbly into this same office to pay his respects!

As I took the general's hand, I noticed that the blue veins were clearly visible through the almost translucent skin—the hands of an elderly man—a fact immediately belied by the firmness of his grip. At that time General MacArthur was sixty-six years of age.

As he greeted me I handed him a copy of my wife's book, *Bombs and Blessings,* supposing that he would accept it, say a few words, and then the interview would be over.

But no. He led me across the room and motioned me to one of the huge leather chairs beside his desk. He sat in another. For ten or twelve minutes he asked questions and then outlined his concept of what the missionaries ought to be doing in Japan. He had given it much thought. His ideas showed he had taken a long look into the future and that his ideas were realistic and practical.

Then, the interview over, I left. But my feet scarcely touched the ground. I had been in the presence of a great man. And yet, every day you and I have the privilege of a personal audience with the God of the universe! He invites us to talk with Him. "Whenever," He says, "under whatever circumstances, don't hesitate. The line is always open." The busier your life becomes, the greater your need to make use of this precious privilege.

After I had been in the ministry for a number of years, I welcomed the chance to visit with my parents on one of our furloughs back to America. One day my father took a well-used little book from the shelf and handed it to me. "Here," he said, "this will increase your efficiency 500 percent!"

I still treasure that book. It is entitled *Power Through Prayer,* by E. M. Bounds. If ever you can get a copy be sure to read it. In simple but forceful langauge it tells how each of us, individually, can really obtain power through prayer.

Perhaps you wonder how you can find time for regular prayer and spiritual exercise. My friend, time spent in communion with your heavenly Father will be the best time investment you can ever make. The wisdom and good judgment that result will bring an efficiency to your life that you have never imagined possible.

Here is one more unique privilege available to you through prayer. Take your frustrations, your disappointments, your bitterness, and even your anger to Him. Sometimes we are afraid to pray the way God wants us to. We ought to tell Him exactly how we feel. Read what David said when he prayed. Some of those prayers are full of vengeful, hateful feelings. But he poured them out to God. And what did God say about David? He called him "a man after my own heart."

So when you have those feelings of hate and bitterness, of frustration and anger, don't bottle them up in your heart. Go to the Lord and say, "Lord, you know how that person treated me. I'm angry! I don't know how to handle him. Lord, You take care of him please." That's the way David prayed.

"That wouldn't be Christian at all," you say. But remember, "Prayer is the opening of the heart to God as to a friend." When you confide in a real friend, one with whom you don't feel any need to hold back, that's the way you talk, isn't it? So pray that way! We wouldn't need so many counselors and psychiatrists if we would talk to God the way He wants us to. Ventilate those inner feelings of conflict. Let God take care of them. That's one of the privileges of prayer—opening the heart to God as to a friend.

Let me suggest that you try increasing your prayer time. I don't say to pray all night. Sometime you may have a crisis that requires that. But if you have been spending ten minutes in prayer, increase it to fifteen and see how it goes. That's not a big amount, is it? Try a little extension of your prayer time and see the difference it will make in your life.

Many, many years ago a very famous engineer named Steinmetz worked for the General Electric Company. He's been dead for a long time now, but he will be remembered as one of the greatest inventive geniuses who ever lived. Much of the electrical wizardry of our day is based on principles he developed. On one occasion he was asked to address a group of engineers. Talking about the opportunities of the future, he said to these men. "Try to find out about prayer."

To a man who had solved so many of the mysteries of electricity, the sources of power available to people who know how to pray presented an enigma. He didn't question the power. He simply wanted to find out how it worked. And that is my suggestion to you. "Try to find out about prayer."

Heavenly Father, we are grateful that in Your divine mercy You have made it possible for us to have instant contact with You. We accept this marvelous opportunity. Teach us to pray. Help us to know how and when to pray. Help us to be unselfish in our prayers. Help us to be earnest and persevering. And then we ask that according to Your will You will answer them. For Jesus' sake. Amen.

---

1. *Gospel Workers,* p. 254.
2. *Steps to Christ,* p. 93.
3. *Ibid.,* pp. 94, 95.
4. *Testimonies for the Church,* vol. 5, p. 214.

Chapter 6
Un-natural Resources

Jesus said: "Follow Me." This is the Incredible Command. It is real. It is directed to you.

In order to follow, you need to see what the Leader does and where He goes. Jesus left the paths clearly marked. We have begun to trace them: first, the Path of Simplicity, and then in our last two chapters we have been considering the Path of Supplication. And now, continuing the same theme, our chapter is entitled "Un-natural Resources."

In following the command that God has given, you will expect to take full advantage of all the natural resources available. God certainly requires this. It isn't fair to expect Him to do something miraculous to overcome inherent laziness on our part, either mental or physical. You will need to be astute, alert, and constantly prepared. You will also need to be informed about what is available all around you in terms of mental equipment, in terms of physical assets, and in terms of opportunity.

But there is an extra, a bonus, if you accept the command, "Follow Me;" for Jesus promises that He will also provide on demand the same resources on which He relied. You must ask for them. That asking is part of the supplication. It is one of the privileges of prayer.

The Bible has much information about this. For now, however, I want to limit my references largely to the book of James, for this apostle has quite a bit to say about prayer. He sums it all up with this simple statement: "The effectual fervent prayer of a righteous man availeth much." James 5:16.

Even if this were all that he said about prayer, it would be a masterpiece. In succinct terms it describes our proper method of access to divine power. But notice some of the other detailed instructions James offers to help you follow Jesus in the Path of Supplication. For instance, He gives this caution: "Ye ask, and receive not, because ye ask amiss." James 4:3. In other words, there may be something wrong with the way you are praying. If you are not getting answers to your prayers, before you blame God, check yourself:

Are you asking with the right motive?

How will the answer you are hoping for affect someone else?

Have you followed God's instructions about your sin problems?

Are you sincere when you say, "Thy will, not mine, be done"?

James also has good news for you. When you come to God sincerely, your sins will all be forgiven. That means He will have a clear channel for fulfilling all of His wonderful promises. These you now have a right to claim.

When you have done all you can, used every natural resource available, then it is your privilege, even your duty, to ask for the other things you need. God has, for the answer to these requests, a vast treasure of un-natural resources. Perhaps we should call them super-natural resources.

One of the finest promises in all Scripture is right here in this book of James. It is especially for people just like you:

> People who face perplexing problems calling for decisions.
> People who are in positions requiring special skills.
> People who must work with difficult individuals or situations.

Here is the promise: "If any of you lack wisdom, let him ask of God, that giveth to all men liberally, and upbraideth not; and it shall be given him." James 1:5.

"If any of you lack wisdom." I can hear you saying, "He's talking about me. That's right where I am."

"Let him ask of God." Notice that you don't get help automatically. The need must be recognized. Then the asking process must be followed.

"Let him ask in faith, nothing wavering." James 1:6.

Have you met these conditions? Then the promise is unequivocal. "It shall be given him." This is the promise of wisdom, the essential ingredient for all problem solving.

My friend, when you are perturbed about which way to take, frustrated because of seemingly unnecessary delays, annoyed and concerned about unexpected difficulties, you have a right to open your Bible to this text. Put your finger on it and say to God, "You said, 'ask.' I'm asking. I don't know what to do. You've said, 'The wisdom will be given.' I claim the promise."

This is part of the Incredible Command. When Jesus says, "Follow Me," the command includes the provision of all that is required in implementing that command. He will not withhold a single thing that is necessary in order to follow Him. All will be given.

Many of your problems will have to do with forces outside of yourself. In other words, you need help that is not ordinarily available. Are you then to give up? Oh, no. For when you have committed yourself to follow Jesus, He promises to make available the resources of heaven itself. That is why I have called this chapter, "Un-natural Resources."

Let us notice again the familiar quotation: "Why should the sons and daughters of God be reluctant to pray, when prayer is the key in the hand of faith to unlock heaven's storehouse, where are treasured the boundless resources of Omnipotence."[1]

These are not supplies that are the result of human genius. These are mental, spiritual, and physical assets on reserve in heaven's inventory! There is never a shortage, never a time when God's materials are temporarily out of stock. And you have the key. Prayer is the key that unlocks that storehouse.

Every once in a while you will find yourself in a situation where natural resources are simply insufficient. You are confronted with a dilemma, a crisis for which you can see no solution. You feel totally helpless. Don't panic! God knows all about your problem. And He also knows what the solution is. He says: "Fear thou not; for I am with thee: be not dismayed; for I am thy God: I will strengthen thee; yea, I will help thee; yea I will uphold thee with the right hand of my righteousness." Isaiah 41:10.

Then take Him at His word. Go to Him and say: "I've done all I can, and it isn't enough. Now I claim Your promise."

Your plea for divine help will not be left unanswered.

"Windows of Heaven"

The Bible uses an interesting term to describe this type of divine intervention. It is called "opening the windows of heaven."

This unique expression does not occur many times in the Bible. In fact, I can find only a few such references. Here they are, in case you want to look them up and read the circumstances involved: Genesis 7:11; 8:2; 2 Kings 7:2, 19; Isaiah 24:18; Malachi 3:10. These, and many other Scriptures, record how God makes available to you and to me His limitless supply of un-natural resources; but these are always given in response to the prayer of faith, to the supplication of each one who has accepted the command, "Follow Me." In your time of desperation, in your moment of great need, these resources are yours to claim.

Does this not give you as a Christian a unique advantage over all other people in the world? It does! Through prayer you can have access to the windows of heaven!

Let me relate a couple of stories that have convinced me beyond any question that God means exactly what He says and that He fulfills His promises.

The apostle James gives us this counsel: "Is any sick among you? let him call for the elders of the church; and let them pray over him, anointing him with oil in the name of the Lord: And the prayer of faith shall save the sick, and the Lord shall raise him up; and if he have committed sins, they shall be forgiven him." James 5:14, 15.

Maybe you have seen something like this happen. Maybe it has happened to you. Once I saw it happen. It took place in Singapore. Along with several other ministers, I participated in a prayer session for a Chinese woman who had been stricken with polio. She was a member of our church and had been in the hospital for several weeks. A daughter who had been attending Union College in the United States had been called home because of her mother's critical condition. The paralysis had advanced until all she could move were her head and her eyes, very slightly.

She and her family had agreed to send for the elders of the church, following the apostle James's instructions. Three or four of us ministers went to her bedside in the hospital. For a few moments we conversed with her and her family. She could not reply, but her eyes showed that she understood. Then we prayed for her, applying the olive oil to her forehead in the anointing service.

She didn't recover instantly. But she began to recover right away. And sooner than anyone had believed possible, she learned to walk again. What a joy it was to see her back in church once again, her face shining with gratitude to her Lord!

She had been in a hospital where most of the nurses were Buddhists. Another member of our church, a woman physician, who was a personal friend of the polio patient, visited her one day in the hospital during her period of rapid recovery. This doctor said to one of the Buddhist nurses, "Do you believe in prayer?"

Reaching for the chart at the foot of the bed, the nurse replied, "Why not?" The record showed many days of spiking fever. The nurse put her finger on one point on the chart. "This is where they had the prayer," she said. "From that point on the fever line leveled out to normal.

This non-Christian nurse needed no sermon on the power of prayer. She had seen it happen. She believed.

Right here I am sure there are some people who would raise one of the following questions:

Question one: "The text you quoted from James says, 'The prayer of faith shall save the sick, and the Lord shall raise him up.' Then why did God not heal my mother but let her die, when her family needed her so much?"

Question two: "I heard one preacher say that in a prayer for healing it is not necessary to say, 'If it is the Lord's will,' for it is always His will that people shall be healed."

These are very sincere questions, and they come again and again from hearts of sincere, earnest people who are devastated at the loss of a loved one. We can consider the two questions together, for they are very much related.

First of all, praying with the provision that the answer be given according to God's will is very much following Jesus in the Path of Supplication. He prayed that way. In the agony of Gethsemane He cried: "Father, if thou be willing, remove this cup from me: nevertheless not my will, but thine, be done." Luke 22:42. The highest expression of faith, the ultimate trust, is to leave the decision with God.

Second, it is not possible for human beings always to know for sure what God's detailed plans are for the future. In His infinite wisdom He may foresee some situation or series of circumstances that, could we have seen as He sees, we would never have made that urgent request, or at the least would have included, "Thy will be done."

Third, the witness before others of willing resignation to God's will on the part of both patient and friends may be a powerful sermon on the mercy, goodness, and love of our heavenly Father. It may also serve as a challenge to others to develop a complete attitude of trust in God.

Of one thing you may be sure: God will always answer every sincere prayer. Sometimes the answer will be Yes; sometimes it will be No; sometimes it will be Wait. But by faith you may rest secure if you leave the final decision to Him. His love for you, His love for those you love, is greater than yours. You can trust Him.

In the very early days of my ministry a fine old man named George Weller used to come to church and sit right down near the front. Afflicted with profound deafness, he would cup his hands behind his ears to try to get something out of the service. He said he rejoiced when I spoke because I talked loudly enough for him to hear a little. I looked forward to seeing George Weller sitting down there, smiling.

The times he inspired me most were when I invited him onto the platform to offer prayer. That man knew his God. He could pray—never a long or tedious prayer—but when he began, it seemed as if he reached out his hand and took hold of the throne of grace. He lived in the presence of God.

One day I arrived at the church on a very wintry Sabbath. George Weller wasn't there. I worried about him, and some of the people told me he had been hurt. After church I drove through snowdrifts to reach his house. This was in the Adirondack Mountains of New York state. The snow was piled on either side of the road as high as the car's roof.

Reaching the Weller house, I knocked on the door, and his wife opened it.

"Hello, Sister Weller. And how is Brother Weller?" I asked.

Just then he came hobbling out of another room. Bent over and obviously in pain, he greeted me heartily, and despite his discomfort, his eyes were bright.

"Brother Weller! What happened to you?"

And then he told me this story:

"I went out in the woods to cut firewood for next winter's supply. I had selected a large tree, and with my axe had cut almost through until it was just about to fall. I wanted to make sure that it fell in the right direction and didn't get caught in the branches of another tree.

"So I went off a little way, cut a small tree, trimmed the branches and made me a pole to use as a lever. I put that pole over my shoulder and started back to the large tree.

"A gust of wind must have caught the branches of the big tree, for it fell before I could get there to direct it. I didn't hear it or see it. It struck me just behind the head, wedged between my head and the pole over my shoulder, and forced me, face down, into the snow.

"I lay there, doubled over, with the weight of that tree crushing me. I couldn't move. The thought went through my mind that somebody would probably find my body in the spring, after the snow melted. And then I remembered, I could pray."

When he reached this point in his story, George Weller looked into my face. Just as simply as a child he said: "I asked my heavenly Father, and He sent an angel and lifted that tree, and let me up."

I believe that is exactly what happened.

George Weller could pray like that. He prayed the kind of prayers God could answer in a sudden moment of desperate need. So although his body still ached from the torn ligaments, his face bore the smile of total trust, and his eyes shone as he told me the story.

As a result of these and many other experiences I don't have to be convinced any more that "prayer is the key in the hands of faith" and that God is able to do "exceeding abundantly above all that we ask or think." Ephesians 3:20. God has the unnatural resources. You simply turn the key.

My friend, those windows of heaven are not limited. You can lift your eyes above the perplexities, the difficult situations, the frustrations, the bitterness, the trials, and the uncertainties. Lift your head a little higher, above them, and by faith you will see the windows of heaven. God is there, ready to open them for you.

When Jesus says, "Follow Me in the Path of Supplication," He means that He is able to open the windows of heaven so you can.

Heavenly Father, we are grateful just now when we realize that the vast resources of Your love are inexhaustible and that they are available to us through prayer. Teach us, Lord, to pray in faith, to pray wisely, to follow Jesus in the Path of Supplication, that we may truly be Your children. We ask this in Jesus' name. Amen.

---

1. *Steps to Christ,* pp. 94, 95.

The Path of Self-Denial

> "Let this mind be in you, which was also in Christ Jesus: who, being in the form of God, thought it not robbery to be equal with God: But made himself of no reputation, and took upon him the form of a servant, and was made in the likeness of men."
> Philippians 2:5-7.

"The life of Christ was one of self-sacrifice and self-denial at every step; and with consistent, Christlike tenderness and love, His true follower will walk in the footsteps of the Master."—Ellen G. White Comments, *SDA Bible Commentary*, vol. 5, p. 1092.

Chapter 7
Watch Out for Number One

"Watch Out for Number One." We've all heard this, or variants of it, such as "You've got to look out for number one," often said with a bit of a smile. But have you ever considered that it is possible to give these expressions another meaning? "*Watch out* for number one!" In other words, "Be careful," because number one may get you into a lot of trouble. Perhaps this is the angle we need to emphasize.

With this thought in mind, consider the following words: "When he had called the people unto him with his disciples also, he said unto them, Whosoever will come after me, let him deny himself, and take up his cross, and follow Me." Mark 8:34.

"Whosoever" includes us all. It makes the command to "Follow Me" a universal one. And here the path in which we must follow is just as clearly defined, "Let him deny himself."

This denial does not imply a loss of self-esteem or some sort of contrived humility. It means taking and maintaining control of your priorities. It means that if you are to obey the command "Follow Me," your own desires, your own plans, your own ambitions must be held in abeyance while you discover what God wants you to do. It also means that you will take time to think of others and their needs before gratifying your own. And now for the perfect example, consider Jesus' life of self-denial.

This requires looking back to a time long before He ever came to this earth. Picture Jesus as a member of the Godhead, eternal with the Father, joining in a council which involved the creation of this world and the inauguration of the human race.

That council determined that man would be made in the image of God and endowed with the power of choice. This meant that man could, and might choose to, turn away from his Creator.

The heavenly council then discussed that frightening possibility. And right there, before the foundation of the world, the plan of salvation was born. The life of self-denial, which characterized Jesus on earth, began in that council. Thus Jesus' life of self-denial began long before He came to this earth.

The apostle Paul wrote: "Let this mind be in you, which was also in Christ Jesus." He continues: "Who, being in the form of God, thought it not robbery to be equal with God." There is no boasting here, no self-assertion. Equality with God is His divine prerogative. But the record continues: He "made himself of no reputation, and took upon him the form of a servant, and was made in the likeness of men: and being found in fashion as of a man, he humbled himself, and became obedient unto death, even the death of the cross." Philippians 2:5-8.

Here we have the ultimate self-denial. Our farthest stretches of human intelligence are insufficient to grasp the significance of this amazing fact—God became man. No extent of human self-denial can even come close to this sublime sacrifice.

"He Lived to Bless Others"

When Jesus came to this earth, He demonstrated in His life that the decision made in heaven would be carried out. This demonstration began early in His youth and continued through His entire ministry. It characterized every part of His action: His work for others, His attitude toward His family, His association with His disciples, His contacts with the religious leaders of the day, His concern for those who followed Him, His compassion for the sick and demon possessed. He identified with all who sought His help, His touch, His word. His was a life of constant self-denial.

Inspiration characterizes Christ's life in a single sentence: "From His earliest years He was possessed of one purpose; He lived to bless others."[1] Here Christ set the example for self-denial. He refused to gratify His own personal desires or His own comfort if it interfered with His objective.

We find a number of these instances recorded in Scripture. Remember the time that Jesus went with His parents to the temple in Jerusalem? When He saw the sacrifice of the lamb, there began to dawn in His heart some perception that He Himself would be the Lamb of God.

After the service, the boy Jesus stayed on in the temple. His parents started for home, thinking that He must be with relatives in the crowd. Night fell before they discovered His absence. It took them a long time, but finally they found Him. He wasn't lost. They had lost Him. To their gentle chiding He replied, "How is it that ye sought me? wist ye not that I must be about my Father's business?" Luke 2:49.

Joseph and Mary did not know what He meant. It is possible He did not fully understand it either. But already He had begun to grasp the thought that His heavenly Father's business would have the number one priority. Right there, as a child, He made the decision that led to a lifetime of self-denial.

Jesus never married and had children of His own. Wasn't that a major self-denial? I'm sure that all the natural instincts in His human heart longed for a family, for a wife, for children. But the care of a family would not conform with His obligations in His heavenly Father's plan. So, He deprived Himself of the comfort they would have brought.

Jesus even subordinated His natural human needs in order to accomplish the task in hand. After the episode with the woman at Jacob's well in Samaria, when the disciples returned with the food they had gone to purchase, He said, "I have meat to eat that ye know not of." Surprised, the disciples said among themselves, "Hath any man brought him ought to eat?" Then Jesus explained: "My meat is to do the will of him that sent me, and to finish his work." John 4:32-34.

Jesus often listened patiently to the tales of woe that people brought to Him. He spent whole nights in prayer. He fasted for forty days as a prelude to beginning His ministry. The things which we sometimes call creature comforts, He gladly laid aside, whenever necessary, in order to get on with His main purpose. Jesus constantly denied Himself because of the moral principle involved. This raises self-denial to its highest level.

58 INCREDIBLE COMMAND

The devil, in his temptation said, "Command that these stones be made bread." Matthew 4:3. He dared Jesus to perform this miracle. Just say the word. There's no need for you to starve! But no. Jesus would not use His divine power to gratify His personal needs.

On one occasion a few of Jesus' over-zealous disciples whipped up the crowd into a frenzy of excitement. They purposed to force Him to bring about a coup d'état against the Roman authorities. The crowd cheered wildly. They wanted Him to assume what they felt was His proper position. John 6:5-21.

To this dangerous crisis Jesus responded with a remarkable display of self-effacing leadership. He persuaded the crowd to disperse and sent the disciples back across the lake in their boat. Bitterly disappointed, they grudgingly obeyed.

On the level of intense personal emotion, Jesus demonstrated an amazing fortitude. He refused to indulge in self-pity. Do you ever remember feeling sorry for yourself? It is a very human, very natural emotion. But I might add, it is an exercise in futility. It does little good, if any, and may cause real emotional harm. Jesus shunned such self-pity.

Near the end of His ministry He tried to prepare the disciples for the events that would lead to His death. Peter determined to do something about it. He took Jesus aside. "Lord," he expostulated, "this shall not be unto thee."

Jesus replied, "Get thee behind me, Satan: . . . for thou savourest not the things that be of God, but those that be of men." Matthew 16:22, 23. Never before had Jesus used a strong expression in talking to Peter. He would not let even His best-loved friends tempt Him into self-pity.

Jesus' great love provided the inspiring motive for it all. He denied Himself because He loved. In the very last moments of His life, as He hung on the cross, His mind numbed with anguish, His eyes blinded with pain, He saw His mother. She was standing with John, the beloved disciple. And for the moment He forgot His own condition. He was concerned for her. From the cross He directed John to take care of His mother. What a beautiful act of love!

My friend, as you consider the completely unselfish life of

Jesus, do you find yourself drawn to Him? Do you say, "I wish I could live like that!"

You *can!*

That's what following Jesus in the Path of Self-Denial is all about. As you study His experience, as you try to pattern your life after His, you will find yourself coming closer each day to reflecting His character. You will feel how much you need His presence in your life. And the more you sense that need, the more real His presence will become. Your life will come to resemble His. Before you recognize what is happening, others will be impressed by the change they see in you.

I recall a personal experience from long years ago. After my first year in college, a couple of friends and I decided we would spend the summer selling religious books in Bangor, Maine. Our plan was to earn a portion of our expenses for the next school year. And, of course, we hoped we could do some good for others in the process. And so it happened that I found myself one day walking along a road doing what students often did—trying to hitchhike a ride. Looking behind me I saw a brand-new Packard approaching. In those days, a Packard rated right up there with the best of the luxury cars!

"I wish he'd stop," I thought—and he did! I climbed in, settled back in the richly upholstered seat, and prepared to enjoy what I thought would be one of my best rides ever.

The driver seemed in a loquacious mood. "What are you doing? Where are you going?"

"I'm a college student," I replied.

"What are you planning to do with your life?"

"I'm attending a Christian school, and I plan to work for the church when I finish."

This seemed to start him thinking. For some time he said nothing. Then, "What would you think of a man who started out with nothing in life, got a job as a common laborer on a construction gang, worked his way up in the construction business, then shifted to automobiles, and by the time he was forty-five years old had made a million dollars. Do you think that man should be happy?"

"Well," I said, "if he came by his money honestly, I suppose he would get some pleasure out of enjoying the things it provided."

He said: "You're wrong. I'm the man who did it. I used to walk down the street in Bangor and look in the window of the jewelry store at those beautiful things when I didn't have in my pocket enough money for my next meal. Now I could go into the place and buy out the whole store, but it doesn't give me any pleasure."

He paused. And you can be sure I didn't say anything!

Then he continued. "Take this car, for instance. I just happened to use this one today. I have a dozen cars in my garage. The only satisfaction I get out of life is what I do for charity."

Another pause.

He turned to me. "Stick with your plan. It sounds like a good one, working for God!"

I am still amazed at the reaction of this wealthy man. I was only a college student, preparing to work for the church someday. But he actually envied *me*! He had learned the hard way that service and self-denial bring life's greatest satisfaction.

In our next chapter we will continue to trace Jesus' experience as He walked in the Path of Self-Denial. We will discover the two motivating factors that led to His lifestyle of total unselfishness.

But for now, will you join me in a moment of prayer?

Heavenly Father, our hearts are captivated by the story of how Jesus gave Himself completely for the good of others. We long to have that same unselfish spirit. Teach us to see how foolish we have been to spend so much time thinking about ourselves. Open our eyes to opportunities for helpfulness and sympathy. Show us how to care. For we ask it in Jesus' name. Amen.

---

1. *The Desire of Ages,* p. 70.

Chapter 8
Giving Up, or Giving In—Why?

When Jesus called His disciples with the Incredible Command, "Follow Me," He did not imply that they should simply copy His every move. He wanted them
>To learn how to think for themselves,
>To develop good judgment of people and of situations,
>To act from principle and not from impulse,
>To know the difference between right and wrong, and
>To share His love for those about them.

He is still the same today. When He calls you to follow Him in the Path of Self-Denial, it is because He knows this is one of the best ways to develop the lifestyle He has designed for you. He also knows that this can be accomplished only when it springs from the proper motives.

Our chapter title, "Giving Up, or Giving In—Why?" leads us into this question of motivation as we continue our study of the Path of Self-Denial. How, for instance, do the world's successful people—athletes, businessmen, scientists, inventors, statesmen—reach their championship status?

Interestingly enough, in nearly every case the record reveals an amazing demonstration of genuine self-denial. For example, consider an athlete seeking Olympic fame. Such an individual will spend many years in unbelievably rigorous training. He will hold to a strict, high-nutrition diet. He will avoid all drugs, narcotics, and alcohol. He will spend countless hours in body-building exercises. He will drill for long periods every day to perfect his special skills. He will keep careful hours for rest. He will give up recreation with his friends, vacations with his family, or any other activity that interferes with his performance ability. These acts of self-denial are done willingly, by choice. Such a person is motivated by his determination to excel.

The same may be said of individuals in business, in politics, in the arts, in the sciences. Their self-denial is real. Their concentration, their single-minded efforts deserve commendation and are often rewarded with outstanding success. These individuals receive the applause of the crowd, the admiration of their friends, as well as the financial rewards of their endeavors. Yet this self-denial, admirable and effective as it is, does not constitute all that is required in accepting Jesus' command: "Follow Me."

Our obedience to Christ must be based on an even higher type of motivation. When we follow Him, it will be not only a system of activities, but also by basing these efforts on the same principles that controlled His life. There are two of these:

Self-denial based on moral principle.
Self-denial based on love.

Self-Denial Based on Moral Principle.

The experience of one of my favorite Bible characters gives some idea of how this kind of self-denial works in the practical affairs of daily living. I refer to Joseph.

We find Joseph, having survived the ignominy of being sold as a slave, serving in Potiphar's household in Egypt. Potiphar, one of Pharaoh's officers, held the position of captain of the guard.

Joseph knew how to work. By strict integrity and repeated demonstrations of dependability, he made himself invaluable to Potiphar. Though technically a slave, he found himself in charge of the whole establishment. Then came the temptation suggested by Mrs. Potiphar. Here was Joseph in the flower of manhood. Imagine the pressure of that temptation.

Besides the natural appeal of sensual gratification, there were other more subtle factors involved. This woman was his master's wife. To yield to her wishes would guarantee him a privileged status of protection. To refuse her could arouse her displeasure and bring swift and severe punishment, and perhaps death. Yet Joseph responded, "How then can I do this great wickedness, and sin against God?" Genesis 39:9. His was an act of self-denial based on moral principle.

Unfortunately this exemplary self-denial has a close counterfeit—self-denial to avoid punishment or inconvenience. Looking at what other people do, we frequently have difficulty deciding from their behavior which of these two ideas really motivates their actions. Sometimes we even mistake our own motives in similar situations.

From teenage days, when I first learned to drive, my foot has always tended to be heavy on the accelerator. Speed limits aroused my resentment. I had an urge to find out how fast every car I drove would really go. But along the way, I discovered traffic officers. This led to driving with one eye on the rear-view mirror. How quickly self-denial of the thrill of speed followed the sighting of a patrol car behind me! Eventually, however, it dawned on me that my outward observation of the speed limit—whenever the police were around—sprang, not from a desire to be a law-abiding citizen, but from a very different motive—the desire to avoid getting caught.

Let's be honest with ourselves. Perhaps we need to take inventory of our motives. In matters of right and wrong, our only safety is to act on the basis of moral principle. Only this will keep us from yielding to the temptations with which we are surrounded.

Christ wants us to follow Him, not to avoid punishment, not for fear of what others may think, not even to receive an eternal reward. But because He wants us to face temptation as Joseph did: "How can I do this great wickedness, and sin against God?"

When World War II broke out, our family was living in the Philippines, along with a number of other Seventh-day Adventist missionaries. When the Japanese occupied the islands, we became civilian prisoners of war. After an initial period in an internment camp, those of us who lived in Manila were allowed a measure of freedom under a form of house arrest. We were permitted to go to our English-speaking church on Sabbath. I happened to be the minister in charge.

A fine Chinese gentleman named L. L. Pan served as one of the local church elders. Mr. Pan was a banker of long experience. He held the position of auditor in the China Bank, one of Manila's largest and most influential banking institutions. He was a faithful Seventh-day Adventist, and not only attended church every Sabbath, but could also preach a fine sermon.

Before the war this China Bank had contributed heavy financial support to Chiang Kai-shek's resistance to Japan's occupation of China. The Japanese had noticed this. So when they occupied the Philippines, one of the first things they did was imprison the officers of the China Bank. Pan was not imprisoned because his position as auditor did not involve the bank's operating policies.

After the Japanese had solidified their control of the Manila metropolitan area, they realized that if any kind of normal business operations were to be resumed, the banks must be opened. They began with the China Bank.

Japanese economic advisors went into the prison for a conference with the officers of the China Bank. They said, "We are going to open your bank. Do you have someone among your employees whom you could recommend to serve as manager under our control?"

This put the bank officers in a tight spot. But while they realized they were in a tight spot, they knew that whomever they recommended to manage the bank would find himself in a far tighter spot. The Japanese would expect such a person to be loyal to them, while at the same time the China Bank officers would expect him to be loyal to them. After conferring among themselves, the bank officers recommended Brother Pan.

When the Japanese came and informed him that he had been selected to manage the China Bank, Brother Pan saw that he faced a very difficult situation. Refusal to accept the appointment could be interpreted as opposition to the occupation forces, while acceptance of the position would be viewed by

GIVING UP, OR GIVING IN—WHY?

many as collaboration with the enemy. In addition to these considerations was another—one that was uppermost in his mind—could he maintain his loyalty to his God and his church, while fulfilling his other obligations? After a brief but fervent prayer, he accepted the challenge.

The Japanese opened the bank with Pan in charge. The bank offered a wide range of banking facilities. It accepted deposits, loaned money, handled checking services. By God's grace Brother Pan walked this precarious tightrope—and he came to church faithfully every week.

One Sabbath morning when he arrived at church, he came to me with a very serious face. "I wish you would have special prayer for me. The Japanese military officer in charge of the bank called me into his office and said, 'Some of the employees have complained that you do not come to work on Saturday. Personally, I don't care whether or not you come in, but it is causing a little problem because the other employees are talking about it.'"

Brother Pan told me he realized he faced a potentially serious problem. Thinking carefully, he told the officer: "I go to church on Saturday."

The officer replied: "I don't mind if you go to church; that is all right. But can't you just stop in at the bank on your way to church and show your face there, then go on?"

I have known some Seventh-day Adventists who would think that this idea offered a good way out. Just stop in, show your face, and then go on. But Brother Pan was made of sterner stuff. He understood self-denial. In the present situation it would almost certainly mean the job, and might even land him in prison.

"Well," Brother Pan responded politely, "if I have to come in on Saturday morning, I'm afraid I'll just have to give up my job."

Pan expected that the next Monday morning he would be called in and told that he had been replaced, or that he might even be arrested and imprisoned. But it didn't happen. Weeks went by. And then one day he came to church on Sabbath all smiles. He told me what had taken place.

The Japanese officer had called him in again. He thought, "Now the ax will fall!" But the officer said: "We have been observing the way you have carried on the operations of this bank. You have done well. Now we are planning to open up two other large banks here in Manila. We have decided to ask you to supervise the operations of those as well."

And so this Seventh-day Adventist became the manager of three of the largest banks in the Philippines, simultaneously, and under very difficult circumstances. Here was a Daniel, if you please. And, like Daniel, he did not hesitate when the moment came for self-denial based on moral principle.

My friend, these moments will come to you—daily—throughout your whole life. When Jesus says, "Follow Me," and looks at you, He expects you also to follow in the Path of Self-Denial. Are you prepared to do that?

Self-Denial Based on Love

Now the other principle involved is self-denial based on love.

There is no higher, no more noble, no more powerful motive. And there is no other secret for a life of acceptable self-denial. Even the incentive we have just considered—denial of self based on moral principle—can only be sustained if our love for God becomes the dominating force in our lives.

Jesus said: "Thou shalt love the Lord thy God with all thy heart, and with all thy soul, and with all thy mind, and with all thy strength: this is the first commandment. And the second is like, namely this, Thou shalt love thy neighbour as thyself. There is none other commandment greater than these." Mark 12:30, 31.

The original act of supreme self-denial comes to us in the words of our favorite Scripture: "God so loved the world, that he gave his only begotten Son." John 3:16. Then Jesus demonstrated the same total love when He died for us. "Greater love hath no man than this, that a man lay down his life for his friends." John 15:13.

Now He says to us: "This is my commandment, That ye love one another, as I have loved you." John 15:12. When our hearts are broken by this amazing love, our response will be, in the

GIVING UP, OR GIVING IN—WHY?

words of the old hymn, "Lord, I give to Thee my life and all to be Thine, henceforth eternally."

Obedience will no longer be a helpless struggle. Duty will be a delight. Service will be a willing offering of gratitude.

Some years ago when we were living in Japan, all the media—television, radio, newspapers, news magazines—carried a veritable fanfare about a social situation that had captured the fancy of the Japanese people, and, indeed, the world. The Crown Prince, Japan's most eligible bachelor, had fallen in love.

For years there had been much speculation about what individual the Crown Prince would eventually marry. Endlessly the news media had surveyed the potential candidates among the peers, the princesses of the numerous branches of Japanese royalty. The Prince himself just didn't seem to be interested in any of them.

Then all at once, in what appeared to be good old American style, the Crown Prince of Japan fell in love with a girl he played tennis with at the summer resort—and she was a commoner.

This presented the imperial family of Japan with one of its most intriguing crises. In 2,600 years of unbroken history, never had the current crown prince married anyone but another member of the nobility. But here was the future emperor making his own selection.

Except for not having royal blood, the girl had every other credential of eligibility. Immediately all the media carried pictures—center spreads and page after page of color shots covering all aspects of her life. Michiko Shoda came from one of the wealthiest families. Her father controlled a great industrial corporation. He would need his wealth if his daughter should actually marry the Prince! The father would be expected to pick up the tab for the wedding!

Then came the announcement of engagement, followed soon after by the setting of the wedding date. As soon as the date for the ceremony became official, the life of this wealthy society girl suddenly went through a remarkable metamorphosis. She found herself in a situation, which in her girlhood days she could not have possibly imagined.

Each day the imperial limousine with its sixteen-petaled chrysanthemum crest on its doors drew up before her father's home. Representatives of the imperial household escorted her to the palace grounds. There she sat at the feet of imperial counselors, learning the protocol of the Japanese court.

She had been a carefree young girl to whom money presented no problem. An excellent education, augmented by wide travel and experience, had given her a sure sense of poise and sophistication. Her stimulating personality had attracted a host of friends. She had led a busy social life, with sports and parties enough to keep any young person absorbed. But now suddenly, it seemed as though almost every moment of her life came under regimentation and strict control. If she decided to go shopping, she couldn't just ask for the family car and head for the Mitsukoshi department store.

She had to notify the imperial household of her plans. They, in turn, notified the Tokyo Municipal Police. The police, in turn, posted guards at every principal intersection on the way from her home to the store. She could not just change her mind and say, "I don't like this store. I'm going to the one across the street." That freedom she had given up when she agreed to marry the Crown Prince. The new life was not easy. But she worked at it.

Then came the wedding day. It captured the attention of the whole nation. Our family decided to stay at home and watch the proceedings on television, rather than to join the several hundred thousand who were lining the route the carriage would take after the ceremony. As the day began, a hundred television cameras covered the event. We began watching at six-thirty in the morning as the imperial limousine drew up in front of the Shoda home. Her family lined up along the entrance to see her off. Mrs. Shoda surreptitiously wiped a tear. The TV cameras caught it all.

After arriving at the palace grounds, Michiko immediately proceeded to the royal chambers to dress for the ceremony. That process took about two hours. She wore thirteen gorgeous kimonos, one over the other.

Her preparations completed, Michiko again appeared on the

GIVING UP, OR GIVING IN—WHY? 69

television screen. We watched in utter fascination. Then came the ceremony itself. The Crown Prince and Michiko were led from the Imperial Palace to a Shinto shrine, maintained for the exclusive use of the royal family. Not even the Emperor himself could enter the inner shrine when the Shinto priest pronounced them man and wife.

But just outside the shrine the imperial family, along with nearly a thousand members of the diplomatic corps, government leaders, official wedding guests representing various nations, and special friends observed the rest of the fascinating procedures.

After a private lunch with the Emperor and Empress, the newly married couple left the palace in a horse-drawn carriage. They proceeded across the famous double bridges that span the moat around the palace grounds and were driven out into the streets of Tokyo.

Television cameras strategically placed kept the entourage in sight for the entire distance as the carriages made their way through the streets to the palace of the Crown Prince. A joyous populace greeted the newlyweds at every point, while millions watched on television. It was one of the happiest days you could imagine.

Michiko Shoda, a commoner, had become the future empress of Japan.

And yet, she had had to give up so much. Her personal freedom had vanished. She couldn't just casually have her friends in any more. She couldn't decide by herself what her plans would be. From now on the imperial household took charge of all these arrangements. She was now the wife of the Crown Prince.

Why did she deny herself the things she formerly enjoyed? Why did she become the wife of the Crown Prince? All of her father's money could not have bought this position. All of her beauty, her intelligence, her lovely and appealing personality could not have purchased her one moment as the wife of the Crown Prince.

It happened for one reason: the Crown Prince loved her. And she loved him. That mutual love made it all possible and worthwhile. It provided the incentive and the reward for the self-denial that was inevitably involved.

And now, my friend, you too may become a member of the royal family, the family of Heaven! For, you see, the Crown Prince loves you!

A lifetime of dedicated effort, a good reputation, a fine family background, a record of unselfish service—not any or all of these can purchase for you the privilege of being a child of God. Only one thing makes it possible. The Crown Prince *loves you*.

And so you hear from His lips the Incredible Command: "Follow Me." He wants you to be a part of His bride, the church. Because He loves you, He wants you to be with Him forever in His eternal kingdom. He promises to make it all possible.

When you fall in love with heaven's Crown Prince, everything that it encompasses becomes a joy. Oh yes, there will be changes in your life. You will turn your back on many of your habits, and perhaps on some of your friends. You will deny yourself and take up your cross and follow Him. But it will be a willing sacrifice, for you are responding to His love.

Are you prepared to follow Jesus in the Path of Self-Denial? You will be if you love Him as He loves you.

Heavenly Father, we thank You that from the depths of divine love salvation's plan has been revealed through Jesus. Our hearts are melted; our resistance is broken down. We realize that the things we must give up, the changes in our lives that must take place, can now be accomplished because we love You truly. May our love in response to Yours prepare us for a place in the heavenly family. For we ask it in Jesus' name. Amen.

The Path of Service

> "He that is greatest among you, let him be as the younger; and he that is chief, as he that doth serve. . . . . I am among you as he that serveth." Luke 22:26, 27.

"Christ gave no stinted service. He did not measure His work by hours. His time, His heart, His soul and strength, were given to labor for the benefit of humanity. . . . To His workers He says, 'I have given you an example, that ye should do as I have done.' "—*Gospel Workers,* pp. 292, 293.

Chapter 9
Whose Priorities?

Jesus said: "Follow Me."

You have already noticed that as you accept the Incredible Command, you will be following Jesus in the Paths of Simplicity, Supplication, and Self-Denial. This trail leads us into the Path of Service. This chapter is entitled "Whose Priorities?"

Jesus came to this world to serve. Said Ellen White, "From His earliest years He was possessed of one purpose; He lived to bless others."[1] Jesus repeated this same thought to His disciples on the night before His death. They were quarreling about who would be the greatest in the kingdom. He put it all into perspective when He said: "Whether is greater, he that sitteth at meat, or he that serveth? is not he that sitteth at meat? but I am among you as he that serveth." Luke 22:27.

From the beginning of His career to His death on the cross, Jesus never wavered from this commitment. He designed His life to be helpful to others. Always He made this his primary objective. He never exalted Himself. He never sought a position that would give Him authority or control. His life of service demonstrated what it means to live for others. That's why He came. That's how He lived.

This in itself is incredible, for He was the Creator. He spoke as one who had authority. All things had been committed into His hands. But on this earth He lived to serve. He proved that those who lead best, serve most. He demonstrated this in all His actions.

Let's take a quick look at Jesus' life of service. There is a temptation to linger a long time on this theme, because it is perhaps the outstanding characteristic of all His work on earth. While we must limit ourselves, we must at least notice the following specific factors about this phase of His ministry.

Christ's life of service knew no limits of time, place, or the status of those He sought to help. He did not keep office hours. I don't mean to imply that office hours are improper for people in the professions or in business. They are certainly essential as guidelines for activity. But it is important to notice that Jesus did not function by the clock. His life of service knew no limit of time.

We find Him, for instance, visiting in Peter's home on a Sabbath. Peter's mother-in-law lay ill. Jesus had been to the synagogue that morning. There had probably been long dialogues with the crowds that followed Him. He needed rest Himself. He also knew that the Jewish leaders were ever quick to accuse Him of breaking the Sabbath when He performed miracles on that day.

Yet, seeing the mother's condition Jesus did not hesitate. He healed her. He didn't consider Himself off duty simply because of the Sabbath, or just because of being a guest in someone's home—nor did He fear the criticism of the Jewish leaders.

Another time, in the midst of His sermon a very unusual thing happened. Suddenly the roof opened up. That would create quite a diversion if it should happen in one of our churches!

Well, on this occasion they lowered a man on a pallet right down in front of where Jesus stood, while He was trying to speak to the assembled crowd. Jesus did not rebuke these men who had interrupted His meeting. His service included attention to the needs of this helpless paralytic. He healed him, told him his sins had been forgiven, and sent him home rejoicing.

Sometimes even during meals, Jesus had to contend with hecklers. At Simon's feast, when Mary anointed His feet, quite a disturbing discussion took place. At the home of Levi Matthew where, by invitation, he participated in a feast with a group of Matthew's friends, whom the scribes and Pharisees described as publicans and sinners, there was an interruption. In response Jesus said to his carping critics: "I came not to call the righteous, but sinners to repentance." Luke 5:32.

His life of service had no limits of location. We find Him on the mountainside, on the sea, walking through the fields, in the synagogues, in people's homes. Wherever He was, if something needed His attention, He gave it. He performed His first miracle at the wedding feast in Cana. In the temple precincts, He drove out the traders and money changers and restored the decorum of that sacred place.

While on a journey with His disciples, He cast out the devils that possessed two demoniacs who rushed out at them from a cemetery. Awaking from sleep in a tossing boat on a stormy sea, He answered the desperate plea of the disciples and stilled the storm.

Jesus recognized no off-limit locations for His services. He was on call wherever He went. And not only this, He drew no distinctions with respect to the status of those who needed His help.

Consider these examples: Jairus, the ruler, whose daughter lay dying. The outcast leper who pressed through the crowd and said, "Lord, if thou wilt, thou canst make me clean." The Roman centurion. The woman of Syrophoenicia. The despised tax collector who climbed into the tree to see Jesus better. The woman with the scarlet past, at Jacob's well.

We also notice that *Jesus' activities covered the whole spectrum of service*. Principally, of course, He healed; He taught; He preached. Apparently He spent more time healing than He did preaching. But in addition to these three main avenues of activity, He also performed a number of unusual services: He turned water to wine; He cleansed the temple; He washed the disciples' feet; He stilled the storm; He fed the multitude. He didn't confine Himself to a job description! Whenever opportunity presented itself, He willingly responded.

And *Jesus served without thought of reward*. He sought nothing for Himself. He gave.

It is true, of course, that people did many things for Him. There were those of comfortable circumstances who provided for His welfare, who helped Him with His food and other needs. The Bible describes some of these people, such as Mrs. Zebedee and several other women who were solicitous of His needs and gave Him financial assistance. But Jesus did not work for these things. He worked because He never forgot His objective.

Jesus also served without regard for His personal feelings. One of the most interesting items in the Bible story of Jesus' life is the record of what happened on the night of His capture in the Garden of Gethsemane.

One of His disciples drew a sword and cut off the ear of a servant of the high priest. Because the other circumstances of this occasion seem so much more important, we often overlook this incident without giving it much thought. And yet, it was one of the most unusual things that happened to Jesus on that memorable night. Here, at the critical moment of His capture, as He bore on His shoulders the weight of the sins of the world, He took time to heal the ear of that unfortunate man.

Picture the scene. The disciples cowering in terror, fearing that they, too, would be taken; the rabble, ready to bind Jesus and lead Him away as a prisoner; those on the edges of the mob who were egging on the more active participants in this ignominious project. And there, in the midst of this turmoil, in the flickering shadows cast by the torches of the mob, Jesus paused to perform His last act of healing, restoring the ear of the high priest's servant!

That tells us something about Jesus. What a compassionate, tender-hearted Man!

A deep sense of urgency also characterized Jesus' life of service. Our chapter title, "Whose Priorities?" leads us to a clear statement made by Jesus Himself, identifying the priorities that controlled His life. "I must work the works of him that sent me, while it is day: the night cometh, when no man can work." John 9:4.

How much we can learn from these words! "I must work." Why did the Creator have to work? Because He had committed Himself. He had chosen a life of service.

What kind of work? "The works of him that sent me." He clarified His priorities for all to hear. Not His desires, not the things that He perhaps would have enjoyed doing. But the works for which His Father sent Him—*these He must do!* And they must be done now, while the opportunity lasts. Jesus never wavered from this priority.

Service Taught by Precept As Well As by Example

Not only by His example, but also in His teachings Jesus defined the meaning of service. Take the experience of His conversation with James and John when their mother brought them before Him with a very special request. I like this story. It helps us understand the character of our Saviour.

Mrs. Zebedee, the mother, had contributed a great deal to the work of Jesus. Not only had she given her two sons to become His disciples, thus disrupting the family fishing business, but she is listed as one of those who ministered to Jesus' material needs.

Considering these facts, it is not surprising that she began to harbor some very motherly ambitions for her sons. Thus she came to Him with the unique request. "Grant that these my two sons may sit, the one on thy right hand, and the other on the left, in thy kingdom." Matthew 20:21.

In the oriental philosophy, a favor carries with it an obligation. Having done so much for Jesus, she felt entitled to ask a favor of Him. So she made her request: "One on thy right hand, and the other on the left." James and John were standing right there. To turn down her request could be embarrassing.

How did Jesus respond?

Here we get a deeper insight into the Saviour's character. He did not chide them. He could have said: "How is it that you have so seriously failed to grasp what My mission is all about? Don't you realize that by coming forward with a request such as this you are earning the enmity of the other disciples? Can't you see that you are making it very difficult, not only for Me, but also for yourselves? Doesn't this demonstrate a lack of the humility everyone should have who follows Me?"

But Jesus said none of these. Instead, He asked them a question. "Are ye able to drink of the cup that I shall drink of?"

"We are able."

Once again Jesus refrained from entering into argument. He said: "Ye shall drink indeed of my cup, . . . but to sit on my right hand, and on my left, is not mine to give, but it shall be given to them for whom it is prepared of my Father." Verses 22, 23.

I'm so thankful that Jesus did not scold those brothers. He didn't rebuke them for their request. Gently He helped them see the importance of genuine service. He helped them see that it is not the position but the commitment that is important. God's will must have top priority.

Continuing our search for what Jesus taught about service, we find five more basic principles:

1. *Singleness of purpose.* "No man can serve two masters." Matthew 6:24. There must be a single devotion, a single loyalty.

2. *Talents are given to be developed.* Study the parable of the talents in Matthew 25:14-30. "Thou has been faithful over a few things, I will make thee ruler over many things."

3. *Sense of responsibility.* In the parable of the lost sheep, the faithful shepherd could not be satisfied with ninety-nine sheep safe in the fold. He went out into the storm until he found the lost one. His sense of duty would not let him rest. Luke 15:4-7.

4. *Importance of small acts of service.* "Whosoever shall give to drink unto one of these little ones a cup of cold water only in the name of a disciple, verily I say unto you, he shall in no wise lose his reward." "Inasmuch as ye have done it unto one of the least of these my brethren, ye have done it unto me." Matthew 10:42; 25:40.

5. *Doing more than is required.* This is sometimes called "second-mile service"—"Whosoever shall compel thee to go a mile, go with him twain." Matthew 5:41.

And so we see that not only with His example, but also in His teachings, Jesus has left clearly marked the Path of Service. His invitation of love, "Follow Me," is also a command to serve.

Our next chapter, "God Wants You!" will give you an opportunity to consider how you will respond when God indicates the

WHOSE PRIORITIES? 79

Path of Service He has specifically designed for you. With this thought in mind, will you join me in a moment of prayer?

Heavenly Father, Thank You for the wonderful example of how Jesus kept His priorities constantly in mind during His short, but so important, life when here on earth. We want to follow Him in this Path of Service. Please show us when and where and how we can work for You. Then give us the wisdom and the courage we will need. For we ask it in Jesus' name. Amen.

---

1. *The Desire of Ages,* p. 70.

Chapter 10
God Wants *You*!

History's record is frequently enlivened with stories of people who have set aside personal ambition, turned their backs on worldly fame, and devoted their entire attention to making the world a little better place in which to live. David Livingstone, Florence Nightingale, Albert Schweitzer, Mother Teresa—to mention just a few outstanding examples. The world has accorded them a fame they did not seek. Not only do we stand in awe of their accomplishments, we envy their strength of character. Their lives challenge us to imitation.

How much greater, then, is the inspiration that comes to us when we study the life of Jesus. We are shamed by His selflessness. We are humbled by His devotion. We are stirred by His accomplishments. And now He says: "I want you! Follow Me in the Path of Service."

What will your response be?

You find a tug at your heart, an eagerness to do something for God. In your enthusiasm, especially if you are young, you may get the feeling that you want to do something really great for God. You will be making a tragic mistake, however, if you have your thoughts focused on some major responsibility to the extent that you overlook the more humble task God has in mind for you. Following Jesus' example includes giving careful attention to these smaller possibilities along the way.

The human nature in us finds considerable fascination in positions and titles. This even happens in the church. We love the sound of titles—president, director, secretary, chairman,

GOD WANTS *YOU!* 81

pastor. We use them in introductions. They are on our letterheads and business cards. They are an important part of our program.

A very wise man in this movement, long dead now, but one who had a major influence on the work of the church, Elder Arthur Spaulding, once wrote an article on this subject. Fortunately, this came to my attention in the early days of my ministry. I still remember one significant passage: "To be a conference president or a home missionary secretary is not very much in the eyes of the world. In God's sight it is nothing at all, except it be as a servant."

What a blessing it will be if, in whatever position or responsibility you may be asked to carry, you can remember that in God's sight it is nothing at all except as it may be another avenue of service. As you follow in this path where Jesus leads the way, consider that whatever service you are able to do, however small it be, is done for God. This provides the nobility.

When I first entered the work of the church, I found myself assigned as a ministerial intern to an experienced pastor and evangelist. I learned a lot from him. He had become an Adventist after working for several years as a newspaperman. He especially looked forward to participating in the church services. Then one Sabbath they asked him to help. They asked him to take up the Sabbath School expense offering!

With difficulty he stifled a feeling of instant resentment. He had been a successful businessman! He had operated his own newspaper! He would have been pleased if they had invited him onto the platform to offer the prayer before the sermon. But to take up the expense offering . . . ?

I heard him tell the story many years later. He caught his emotions in time. "If this is where I start," he said to himself, "then I better get on with it." And with a smile, he passed the plate. He had successfully met one of God's important little tests.

This man became a fine minister. When I worked with him, he had a district of six churches. Later he accepted appointment as a conference president and gave many years of excellent service. But he never forgot that early experience.

Anything that we do for God carries with it its own nobility.

How Will God Lead?

You ask, "How will I know what I can do for God?" This brings the problem right down to where you live.

My answer is, "If you really want to know, if you are willing to do whatever God wants you to do, He will surely lead you to that task."

Consider these familiar words: "Every true disciple is born into the kingdom of God as a missionary."[1] Notice that this equates the duties of service with the conversion experience. And then we have another wonderful statement: "Not more surely is the place prepared for us in the heavenly mansions than is the special place designated on earth where we are to work for God."[2]

This is one of our best-loved quotations. I believe what it says. I know it is true. But where is that *special place*.

No doubt you have given this question serious thought. What does God want me to do? If you will maintain this search as the basis for your choice of priorities, you will make no mistake. God will lead you. He will help you find what you ought to do, what He wants you to do. However, He may lead you through a series of varied responsibilities on the way to that special place He is holding. And some of His leadings may come in ways you did not expect.

Right now I am letting my mind go back to my sophomore year in college. That was during the Great Depression. Conditions in our country were such as most of you have never seen. You could scarcely imagine them. People with doctor's degrees stood in breadlines. They couldn't even find a job digging ditches.

As a young college student, I had started thinking seriously about what I would be doing when I finished. My father, a Seventh-day Adventist minister, hoped I would want to be a preacher too. But somehow I just didn't see it that way. I wanted to work for God, no question about that. But I thought I wanted to be a teacher, not a preacher. So I planned my college course with that in mind. I weighted it heavily toward the liberal arts, a major in religion, a major in history, a minor in English.

Then I had some other things in mind. "When I finish college," I thought, "if there are four or five different things I can do, I'll have a better chance of getting a job in one of our academies somewhere." I had been working in the printing department for some time, so I figured I could handle an academy print shop. Then, always interested in music, I had begun the piano conservatory course, what is now called a music major. I felt I had it figured out pretty well. If I could do music and printing, besides being able to teach religion, history, and English, I surely should be able to get a job somewhere.

And then I met a girl.

It frequently happens in college, you know. I liked that girl very much. She had something I felt I needed. We met working together on the school paper. We shared our musical interests. As the days went past I began to think that I had pretty much concluded my search for the girl of my dreams.

One day as we were walking together, she dropped a casual remark. She said, "I've always thought I would like to marry a minister." She didn't state it as an ultimatum. She didn't urge me to think about it. She didn't press the subject at all. She simply remarked, "I've always wanted to marry a minister."

Now I'm not ashamed to say that God used that method to get through to me with a call to the ministry. She had no idea of the inner turmoil she had begun for me. But that remark of hers started me thinking very, very seriously, wondering if perhaps I had really been pursuing the right plan for my life. As this turned over and over in my mind, I became convinced that God did indeed want me to change my whole study program and take the ministerial course.

This took some doing. Already two years into my college work, to change courses and still finish in four years presented a major problem. But at the end of that sophomore year, I made the change. Incidentally, I married the girl—the smartest thing I ever did! As I write, we have been married very happily for fifty-three years!

84 INCREDIBLE COMMAND

You see, the Lord finally got through to me with His priorities. "This is what I want you to do"—and it wasn't what I had been planning. I have never been sorry, even for a moment. God wanted me to do something different from what I had in mind, and I am glad He let me know it. God will do the same for you, for anyone who is sincere in saying, "Not my priorities, but Yours."

The apostle Paul, when he was still called Saul, already into his professional career, a brilliant young legislator with a future assured, suddenly found himself confronted on the road to Damascus with glory from the throne of God. He saw Jesus. The Incredible Command came to him, "Follow Me." In that moment of stricken blindness but opened spiritual vision, Saul said, "Lord, what wilt thou have me to do?" Acts 9:6. Suddenly his priorities were in order.

God then led him step by step. It took a long time. If you are a little frustrated in your career and wonder how things are working out for you, just study the record of the years that passed between the time God called Saul on the road to Damascus and the time when he actually began his ministry in Antioch. Those are fascinating years. You'll find they were also very frustrating.

Here was this brilliant man, but the brethren were not about to accept him. When he went to Jerusalem and started preaching, people listened. Persecution began to boil again. The brethren called him in and said: "Now, Saul, you are a great man and a fine preacher, but you are rocking the boat. You better go back to your home in Tarsus until things settle down. Don't call us. We'll call you."

Paul felt rejected. But he kept his priorities clear. He went back to Tarsus and made tents for a while. And he waited.

Finally, the Lord said, "Now is the time." Barnabas came and found him. "We've got something going over in Antioch. Come on over and help us." It was not the call he had expected. It didn't come from the brethren. Some earnest people a long way from headquarters had started a lay program in Antioch, and the invitation came through them. But Saul did not hesitate. He recognized the answer to his priority questions: "Lord, what wilt thou have me to do?" He packed up and went to Antioch with Barnabas. God had finally led Saul, the great persecutor, all the way around to Paul, the great missionary.

Now, my friend, if you are puzzled about your future, if you are wondering what kind of work God wants you to do, remember that all you need to do is to step out and accept the Incredible Command, "Follow Me." Then God will lead to what He has planned for you.

I have no idea what God may have in mind. Maybe He wants you to be an engineer, a mechanic, a secretary, a school teacher, or a farmer. Maybe He wants you to be a nurse, a lawyer, a business person, or a homemaker. All of these are noble and proper. He may also have planned some special little niche of service that just fits your abilities and personality. Whatever it maybe, if it is God's priority for you, that's exactly what you ought to do. If you ask Him, He will show you.

But remember, He has His own schedule and His own methods of revealing His will. He may do it by closing doors, instead of opening them. He may do it by not saying "go" or "stay," but "wait."

He is much more patient that we, so "wait" is one of His most frequent answers to our prayers. But if that is God's priority for you for the moment, then waiting is what you ought to do. "They also serve who only stand and wait."[3] The sincerity of your commitment is the measure of God's response to your request for His leading.

When you ask God to help you know how you can serve, you have the right to claim His promise: "Thine ears shall hear a word behind thee, saying, This is the way, walk ye in it, when ye turn to the right hand, and when ye turn to the left." Isaiah 30:21. When He shows you the way and then says, "Follow Me," with that command will come all the enablings you need to obey.

Dear God:
  I do not ask for mystic glimpse of heavenly light;
  Nor for a voice to echo down from vaulted skies.
    I only ask for this;

That as I face the future, baffled and afraid,
Within my heart Thy still small voice shall speak and say,
"Fear not, this is the way!"[4]

---

1. *The Desire of Ages,* p. 195.
2. *Christ's Object Lessons,* p. 327.
3. John Milton, "On His Blindness."
4. Paul H. Eldridge.

The Path of Suffering

"He is despised and rejected of men; a man of sorrows, and acquainted with grief." Isaiah 53:3. "Christ also suffered for us, leaving us an example, that ye should follow his steps." 1 Peter 2:21.

"Christ's mission could be fulfilled only through suffering. Before Him was a life of sorrow, hardship, and conflict, and an ignominious death. He must bear the sins of the whole world. He must endure separation from His Father's love."—*The Desire of Ages,* p. 129.

Chapter 11
Pain Threshold, Endurance Limit

Jesus said: "Follow Me!" Within this command there is implied all the strength, all the talent, all the facilities required to obey. You have noticed that if you are to accept this challenge, if you are to follow Jesus, it is necessary for you to give careful attention to how He walked when He was here on this earth, for it is obvious that if you are to follow Him, it will be walking in the human footsteps He left for us.

Jesus walked the Paths of Simplicity, of Supplication, of Self-Denial, and of Service. Looking ahead, you may wish you could somehow avoid this one. It is the Path of Suffering. But here, as in the others, Jesus does not hesitate. "If you would come after Me," He says, "you must follow Me also in the Path of Suffering."

Our topic for this chapter is "Pain Threshold, Endurance Limit." We want to notice a large number of texts, so may I suggest you have your Bible ready beside you as we proceed. The first text is found in Hebrews 2:10.

Notice that this is talking about Jesus. But what it says about Him is something we do not always consider. It is important. "It became him, for whom are all things, and by whom are all things, in bringing many sons unto glory, to make the captain of their salvation perfect through sufferings."

Christ lived the only perfect life. You wish you could live as He lived. But the sad fact is that every human being has failed. And yet this remarkable Scripture indicates that the sufferings which Jesus endured helped Him maintain His perfect record.

Consider two other verses: "Though he were a Son, yet learned he obedience by the things which he suffered." Hebrews 5:8. "Hereunto were ye called: because Christ also suffered for us, leaving us an example, that ye should follow his steps." 1 Peter 2:21. These scriptures make it very clear that the command "Follow Me!" involves the Path of Suffering, as well as the other paths which Jesus walked.

The fact that Jesus learned through suffering may help you understand why you have so many troubles. We want to talk about that in this chapter. What is your threshold of pain? What is your endurance limit? Why is suffering necessary?

Jesus: "A Man of Sorrows, and Acquainted With Grief"

As in each of our previous chapters, let us consider first of all the example Jesus has left for us. Notice carefully the way in which He dealt with the many different types of anguish He experienced. He endured the ordinary human woes. We find Him sitting by Jacob's well in Samaria, feeling both hungry and thirsty. He was also tired. The regular toils of daily living resulted in normal fatigue for Jesus. So He understood these simple human experiences of discomfort and pain.

Jesus also suffered in sharing the problems of others. This is an amazing kind of anguish, but very real. The sympathetic, compassionate sharing of what others feel is something parents understand. But Jesus knew more about this than anyone else has ever learned. We find many instances of this recorded in Scripture, all of them beautiful. I like the one of the two blind men. Jesus, walking along surrounded by crowds, as usual, heard these two blind men crying, calling for Him to help them.

"Have mercy on us, O Lord, thou son of David."

These men thought this might be their only chance. Never again might they be so close to the One they had heard could heal. Now He seemed to be passing them by. In desperation they raised their voices above the clamor of the multitude.

"Have mercy on us!"

The people in the crowd, annoyed, said, "Keep quiet; you're disrupting things. Be still!"

But Jesus heard. The cry of desperation never fails to reach His heart. So He stopped. He called those two men to His side. You can imagine the whole crowd coming to a halt and then opening a path so the blind men could get through to Jesus.

"What will ye that I shall do unto you?"

"Lord, that our eyes may be opened."

"So Jesus had compassion on them, and touched their eyes: and immediately their eyes received sight, and they followed him." Matthew 20:30-34. "He had compassion." Over and over again we find this expression.

The multitudes came around the lake to where He and His disciples had gone for a private outing. They thronged around Him. They broke up His little plan for some quiet recreation with His disciples. But the record says: He "was moved with compassion toward them, because they were as sheep not having a shepherd." Mark 6:34.

So often that sympathy showed through. And this constant care and thoughtfulness for others exacted a physical and emotional toll on Him. Jesus suffered vicariously the feelings of those who were in anguish around Him. He repudiated, however, the theory that specific suffering came as the result of punishment for sin.

This was a common belief held by the Jewish people. Any time anyone suffered, they believed it resulted either from his sin or the sins of the parents. A number of incidents show how Jesus refuted this supposition. He showed that much suffering comes upon all, and He shared that human anguish. What a pitying, loving Saviour!

But on another level, one of keen physical pain, Jesus suffered torture. Not many of us have had an experience comparable to His. He was beaten, scourged, nailed to the cross. And even as His life ebbed away, He wore a crown of thorns. He suffered the agony of an extremely painful death. He was "a man of sorrows, and acquainted with grief." Isaiah 53:3.

Yet all of this did not produce His keenest anguish. He experienced mental suffering such as we can never know. Not only at the time of His death, but throughout His life Jesus knew the bitterness of scorn, disbelief, ingratitude, rejection, and hatred.

Any psychologist will be quick to point out that mental suffering can be even more acute than physical pain. Jesus understood this. It constituted His greatest source of discomfort.

Jesus Lived With Disappointment

Let us notice a few of the occasions and circumstances under which Jesus suffered mental anguish. He lived with disappointment. Disappointment because His own people refused to accept Him. "He came unto his own, and his own received him not." John 1:11. Disappointment with the Jewish leaders. They turned away from Him, even though He was the Rock, the Chief Cornerstone, on which the whole spiritual temple must be built.

Consider the sad, but beautiful, picture of what happened at the time of Jesus' triumphal entry into Jerusalem. Some of you may have visited the Holy Land, as I have, and have seen the place where the triumphal entry occurred. From the vicinity of Bethany you come over the crest of Olivet, and there, across the valley, lies the city of Jerusalem. It is a marvelous view even today. More magnificent in Jesus' time than it is today, the view from the Mount of Olives took in the breathtaking picture of Herod's temple, that superb white marble masterpiece of architecture that had taken forty-six years to build.

On that day, accompanied by a multitude who were shouting His praises, Jesus paused on the Mount of Olives with the city spread out before Him. The crowd beheld with amazement as He wept over the city. In that agonizing moment He said: "If thou hadst known, even thou, at least in this thy day, the things which belong unto thy peace! but now they are hid from thine eyes." Luke 19:42.

On another occasion He exclaimed: "Oh, Jerusalem, Jerusalem, thou that killest the prophets, and stonest them which are sent unto thee, how often would I have gathered thy children together, even as a hen gathereth her chickens under her wings, and ye would not! Behold, your house is left unto you desolate." Matthew 23:37, 38. His rejection by His own nation nearly broke His heart.

PAIN THRESHOLD, ENDURANCE LIMIT 93

Jesus suffered keen disappointment because of His disciples. He lived with them. He ate with them. He slept with them. He walked the roads of Palestine with them. He shared with them His most intimate thoughts, His plans, His objectives. And yet they failed to understand. He had talked plainly and patiently with them about the future. They simply could not grasp the nature or the principles of His kingdom.

In sorrow He asked, "Are ye also yet without understanding?" Matthew 15:16. A gentle chiding, but it revealed His disappointment that these men whom He had tried to reach with a comprehension of His purpose had failed to grasp it.

The loss of Judas brought great disappointment to Jesus. Strange, in a way, for He had not invited Judas to begin with. Judas had volunteered, "I will follow thee, whithersoever thou goest." And Jesus let him come. Jesus kept trying to get through to Judas. His last attempt came when He knelt before Judas and washed his feet. But Judas would not yield. A few moments later he rose from the communion table and went out into the night to complete his deal for the betrayal of his Master.

For some of Jesus' greatest suffering we must consider His amazing struggle in the Garden of Gethsemane. In *The Desire of Ages,* pages 685-697, you will find the most poignant and beautiful description ever written of Jesus in the Garden. It was there that Jesus faced the greatest chance for failure in the whole history of the plan of redemption.

On many occasions during His ministry, Jesus had been accused of serious wrongdoing. His enemies had charged that He had a devil, that He blasphemed His Father's name. They even insinuated that He was illegitimate. And though all these accusations were false, they had caused Him mental anguish. He had survived because He had no guilt of His own.

But now, as He prayed in Gethsemane, there began to sweep in on His soul the awful sense of carrying the guilt for the sin of the whole world. He feared that the separation from His Father which this vicarious weight of guilt would bring might make him too weak to resist the final temptation of Satan.

This was the cup He feared to drink. Over this decision He shed drops of blood. Here the whole plan of salvation could have failed. Instead, victory came as Jesus prayed. He made His irrevocable decision to go through with the cross.

And so the path of personal suffering which Jesus walked led inevitably to the cross. There His anguish, both physical and mental, reached its climax. As He hung on the cross, the shadows crept in closer yet. He had dreaded most of all the sense of being separated from His Father.

Bearing the guilt of the whole world, He felt every bit of the anguish of those who are eternally damned. Heart broken, He cried: "My God, my God, why hast thou forsaken Me?"

Could there be any greater grief than this?

Suffering: A Learning Process

Friend, this loving, compassionate, suffering Saviour knows all about your grief. So it is with infinite sympathy that He says: "Follow Me in the Path of Suffering."

It is obvious, then, that in your commitment to follow Him, you must expect that some suffering is sure to be your lot. There is no promise that you can go though life without it. Normal discomforts, sickness, accidents, disappointments, loss of loved ones—all of us have known some of these misfortunes. You may feel you have had more than your share!

In our human frailty we will never on this earth be able to understand how God divides the amount of suffering He permits to come. However, there is one remarkable passage back in the Old Testament which offers comfort. It implies that God measures the amount of anguish that will be permitted to come to any one of us by our individual ability to withstand it.

When God commanded Israel to destroy the cities that obstructed their conquest of the Promised Land, He gave instruction about handling the booty which they would seize. They were told to put these items through a purifying process which also had a ceremonial purpose. The metal objects were to be passed through fire. The things which were not made of metal, which could be damaged by fire, were to be purified by water. Numbers 31:21-23.

God deals the same way with human beings. I heard of one little old lady who said: "I know God never lets me have trials that are greater than I can stand; but I sometimes wish He didn't have so much confidence in me!" We do get that feeling. You may be tempted to say, "The Lord is trying to make me think I'm metal when I'm really only cloth!"

Remember, friend, God knows you better than you know yourself. The promise is: "God is faithful, who will not suffer you to be tempted above that ye are able; but will with the temptation also make a way to escape, that ye may be able to bear it." 1 Corinthians 10:13.

Worry or Trust?

Much of our mental suffering results from worry. God wants us to transfer this to trust. Jesus said: "Take no thought, saying, What shall we eat? or, What shall we drink? or Wherewithal shall we be clothed? . . . For your heavenly Father knoweth that ye have need of all these things. But seek ye first the kingdom of God, and his righteousness; and all these things shall be added unto you." Matthew 6:31-33.

This comes from the Sermon on the Mount, that beautiful passage where Jesus tells about the birds and the flowers and Solomon's glory and how much greater is God's care for you. He does not mean that you should not make any plans for the things you need. But He does mean that when you have done your best, you should have less anxiety and more trust.

Fear of what may happen in the future is one of the greatest causes of mental suffering. I remember during World War II in the Philippines, we had been temporarily released from the prison camp and were living under a house-arrest sort of arrangement. Actually we were in considerable danger. In the internment camp we were at least protected from anything that might be the result of the fighting itself. But outside the camp, living in a compound of private houses, we were at the mercy of any passing soldier.

There were some people on our compound whom I thought had too much courage. Although the occupying Japanese army had banned all shortwave receiving radios, some of our folks rigged up a radio so they could listen on shortwave to the news broadcasts from America. There were Japanese civilians living in a house that looked right into our compound.

The presence of this radio really bothered me. I thought, "Here these folks are, doing something that is clearly against the law, something that could lead at the least to imprisonment or even worse. If they should get caught it would involve the whole compound!"

Ten families lived in five houses. (By the way, that makes for a different sort of anguish! But that's another story!) I spent hours mulling over this problem. I knew about the radio. If any Japanese came to investigate, they would talk to me because I was the only one who spoke Japanese.

Over and over again I said to myself, "I don't believe in this. I don't like it. It's risky. I wish they would stop. And I'll be the first one to get in trouble!" I tossed on my pillow through many sleepless hours, wondering what I would say when the Japanese military police came to check it out.

Nobody ever came. All of my anxiety, and believe me it was real, was an exercise in futility. Nothing but wasted worry. That's true with most of our worry. It is a waste of mental effort. It is anguish that we really shouldn't be feeling.

Having said all this, we must recognize that we will inevitably be faced with much suffering that we did not invite and which we cannot escape. When that happens, God wants us to turn to Him for help. You need not hesitate. Even if you have done something which contributed to the problem, God will not ignore your earnest and repentant prayers. He is "our refuge and strength, a very present help in trouble." Psalm 46:1. But the persistent question keeps coming: Why? What purpose is served by all this anguish? In our next chapter, "Why *Me, Lord?*" we will consider this nagging problem. But, for now, will you join me in prayer?

Heavenly Father, our hearts have been touched with the thought that even Jesus learned something from suffering. This gives us courage. We still often wonder why, but please help us to be patient and learn, even as we follow Jesus in the Path of Suffering. For we ask it in His name. Amen.

Chapter 12
"Why Me, Lord?"

As you continue to consider the meaning of following Jesus in the Path of Suffering, do you feel a sense of foreboding, even fear? Do you find yourself resenting the anguish you experience so often? Do you cringe at the apparent inevitability of pain. Does it seem unfair?

You are not alone. This is one of the Christian's most perplexing dilemmas. The very best thing you can do about it is to go God with the questions. Ask Him what it all means. Get Him to tell you how to face each test of anguish when it comes.

God has never said you will have no suffering. But He wants you to understand the causes. He points out the lessons you can learn. He also promises that in every cloud of pain, you will find a rainbow of courage. He guarantees to help you endure what you cannot avoid.

Someday you may actually suffer persecution. The apostle Paul makes a flat statement: "All that will live godly in Christ Jesus shall suffer persecution." 2 Timothy 3:12. Does this frighten you? It does me! But Christ has given some wonderful assurance: "Ye shall be hated of all men for my name's sake: but he that endureth to the end shall be saved." Matthew 10:22. Following Christ when such persecution comes will be easier to bear, I believe, than many other kinds of anguish.

There is a danger, however, that you may by injudicious actions bring persecution on yourself. Is it possible that in your natural desire to justify yourself you may imagine that some suffering is persecution when it is really a punishment you deserve? The apostle Peter, who had a good deal of experience with suffering, gives us some very wise counsel: "It is better, if the will of God be so, that ye suffer for well doing, than for evil doing." 1 Peter 3:17. In other words, if you must suffer, it better be from persecution for something good rather than as punishment for something bad! That makes sense, doesn't it?

Peter elaborates: "Let none of you suffer as a murderer, or as a thief." To which we might reply with some self-assurance, "At least I won't have to worry about that!" But notice the rest of the text: "Or as an evildoer, or as a busybody in other men's matters." 1 Peter 4:15. Now that's getting closer to where we live! And the apostle indicates that this is pain from deserved punishment and therefore is really self-inflicted.

Elsewhere Peter puts the problem in perspective: "What glory is it, if, when ye be buffeted for your faults, ye shall take it patiently? but if, when ye do well, and suffer for it, ye take it patiently, this is acceptable with God." 1 Peter 2:20.

Persecution may come, but it should never be because we have invited it. I have known of young men in the military services who, by their actions and attitudes have literally invited harassment for their faith. With a little more careful handling of the situation they could have reached an understanding with their commanding officer.

That's what Jesus meant when He said: "Be ye therefore wise as serpents, and harmless as doves." Matthew 10:16. He also told His disciples, "When they persecute you in this city, flee ye into another." Matthew 10:23. In other words, don't invite persecution. Don't invite problems that could be avoided.

Now I can hear someone say: "I think I understand the part about persecution. I'm willing to leave that in God's hands. But what about the suffering that comes from sickness, accidents, family problems, misunderstandings, and unfair treatment?"

The agonizing questions continue: "Does God inflict suffering? And if He doesn't, why does He permit Satan or our enemies or circumstances to cause us so much anguish? And why do things sometime seem to pile up one upon another until I can't stand it any longer?"

If this is how you feel, don't despair. Give God a chance to answer.

Lessons From Pain

God points out to you gently that suffering does have value. He wants you to remember that although you may not be to blame for your suffering, He does permit it, and for various reasons. But the suffering itself is the result of living in a world controlled temporarily by Satan, the originator of all pain.

True, man voluntarily surrendered this control to Satan when the first sin took place. But the infliction of anguish has been one of the devil's most potent weapons ever since. If God did not hold over you His protecting hand, your sufferings would be infinitely greater than they are.

Consider the experience of Job. In his story inspiration gives us the clearest Bible picture we have of the source and meaning of suffering. Some biblical scholars feel that the book of Job is the oldest book of the Bible. It should give you some comfort to know that the very first gift of divine revelation in Scripture came to mankind to give an answer to the problem of pain in relation to the love of God. Thus, from a psychological standpoint, the story of Job is one of Scripture's most therapeutic portions. Consider some further references which help you understand the value of suffering.

First, *the presence of suffering in the world is a constant demonstration of the awfulness of sin.*

Have you ever thought, "If God is a God of love, why is the world so full of agony?" Listen to the apostle Paul: "We know that the whole creation groaneth and travaileth in pain together until now." Romans 8:22. This is Satan's work. Nature suffers, people suffer, animals suffer, the environment suffers. And if there had never been any sin, there would never have been any suffering.

In God's love and gentleness He has led you to realize that suffering not only reminds you that you are living in the kingdom of sin. It also creates a great longing to exchange this evil world for the kingdom of righteousness—and God promises to see you through this transition.

Second, *suffering also teaches obedience and repentance.*

You read about Christ as the Captain of your salvation, learning obedience through the things that He suffered. This fully qualifies Him to say: "As many as I love, I rebuke and chasten: be zealous therefore, and repent." Revelation 3:19. God allows you enough pain to help you recognize your mistakes. He loves you. And so He rebukes you, just as a child is corrected by a parent who loves him dearly.

God knows there are times when suffering may serve to teach important lessons. Very, very early in life one discovers that doing forbidden things results in some kind of discipline from parents. And that kind of suffering seems to be beneficial! Says the wise man, Solomon, "Foolishness is bound in the heart of a child; but the rod of correction shall drive it far from him." Proverbs 22:15. So there seems to be good Scripture for the idea that a little well-conditioned anguish administered at the right time, in the right spirit, and under proper circumstances has a therapeutic effect!

As you have grown older, and attained a higher level of sophistication, it still follows that if you do something wrong, you may expect to suffer the anguish that goes along with it. And, of course, that includes the mental anguish which may actually be worse than the physical.

Here is another text: "Godly sorrow worketh repentance to salvation not to be repented of: but the sorrow of the world worketh death." 2 Corinthians 7:10.

A year or so after I went to college, I had occasion to go back and visit my old academy. There's something nostalgic about seeing again the place where you spent your most impressionable years. I arrived there during Christmas vacation.

As soon as I stepped on campus I sensed a strange atmosphere. Most of the students had gone home for vacation, but those who were around seemed to be talking in a subdued tone. I ran into one of my old friends, and he filled me in with what had happened.

One of the teachers who had been at that school for a long time, a man I had known very well, had gone into his garage, attached a hose to the exhaust pipe of his car, and had run the hose through one of the car windows. Being a science teacher, he had known exactly what he was doing. Then he had climbed into the car, rolled up all the windows and started the engine. In a few minutes he was dead—a suicide.

My friend took me into the school library. There, across one corner of the reading room, the teacher's body lay in its casket. They were getting ready for funeral services that afternoon.

How could it have happened? Why?

Then the sad story came out. This teacher had been involved with one of the girls in the school. They had been discovered together. He couldn't face the consequences of his actions. Instead of the sorrow that leads to repentance, he had been overwhelmed with the sorrow of the world that leads to death. But, thank God, there is a godly sorrow that leads to repentance!

A third value of suffering: *It teaches endurance.*

A number of years ago as I walked along a street in Osaka, Japan, not far from our evangelistic center, I came to a place where they taught karate. As you know, that is one of the very popular oriental arts of self-defense. In front of this karate classroom, I discovered a very simple bit of training equipment—a post, driven into the ground. Fastened to the post was a crude padding of matted straw. This padding, not very thick to begin with, had been worn nearly all the way through to the wood.

It had been worn by the students of karate. Each one had stood beside it and slammed the edge of his hand against that post time after time after time. This exercise, repeated daily, permanently deadened the nerves and turned the edge of the hand into a hard-calloused weapon, a weapon that could literally kill if used against the vulnerable parts of an opponent's body.

Why did these ambitious young fellows undergo such grueling training? They endured suffering to achieve a goal.

You don't have to go to Japan to see this kind of training punishment. Every football game demonstrates it. Or watch a boxer with his punching bag or sparring with a partner in a ring. These painful exercises tend to strengthen the individual. He gains endurance. This suffering gives him something he knows he needs. And he endures the pain because he wants to win.

Listen to the apostle Paul: "I therefore so run, not as uncertainly; so fight I, not as one that beateth the air: but I keep under my body, and bring it into subjection: lest that by any means, when I have preached to others, I myself should be a castaway." 1 Corinthians 9:26, 27. And then he sums it all up: "Our light affliction, which is but for a moment, worketh for us a far more exceeding and eternal weight of glory." 2 Corinthians 4:17.

God knows that you can learn to resist evil by the same kind of training. He knows that the exercises of suffering will prepare you to endure persecution and all the other trials that may be ahead. He lets the little sufferings come along the way so that when the big tests arrive you will be able to stand. You will triumph because you have learned through the things which you have suffered.

Heavenly Father, we are grateful that Jesus, our Example, our Commander, left us reasons to understand the sufferings that come. Teach us to endure. Increase our strength. Help us learn the lessons we need to learn from the anguish we face. And then give us the courage to follow wherever Jesus leads, even though it be through the Path of Suffering. For we ask it in His name. Amen.

The Path of Sacrifice

"Greater love hath no man than this, that a man lay down his life for his friends." John 15:13.
"Even Christ our passover is sacrificed for us."
1 Corinthians 5:7.

"Looking upon the crucified Redeemer, we more fully comprehend the magnitude and meaning of the sacrifice made by the Majesty of heaven. The plan of salvation is glorified before us, and the thought of Calvary awakens living and sacred emotions in our hearts."—*The Desire of Ages,* p. 661.

Chapter 13
Love Without Limit

Jesus said: "Follow Me!" This is the Incredible Command.

Even after the study you have already given to this divine invitation, does it still sometimes seem beyond human possibility to obey? You have felt yourself drawn by the Saviour's powerful personality. You have been inspired by His example, by His unique lifestyle. You really want to make a commitment, step out, and follow Him.

Faced with this challenge, your intellect admits that God has promised to provide all the wisdom, courage, aptitude, and facilities you will need. Is there something that still seems to hold you back?

I believe you will find the answer to these hesitations as you turn the next few pages. You will see that God extends His hand to you. He says, "You don't need to know all that the future holds. Come along with Me. I'll be with you all the way."

Our chapter title is "Love Without Limit." Here we will enter one of the most significant paths where Jesus walked, the Path of Sacrifice. At the outset, let us first consider what is implied by the word *sacrifice*. It has a double application. It means "giving up something of value for an even higher good," "offering something as a tribute of praise or as an atonement."

When Jesus left His position in the courts of heaven to come to this earth, that action represented an almost inconceivable sacrifice. But in addition, we must consider how this concept revealed itself also in His life here on earth.

We have already noticed how much He gave of Himself, of

His time, of His emotional resources for the benefit of those around Him. All of these He gladly offered for what He had determined as the higher good—the salvation of the human race. And then, on the cross, He fully met the other meaning of sacrifice. He offered His own life as an atonement for sin. This proved, not only to the whole world, but also to the entire universe, that indeed His love was without limit.

Sacrifice Defined by Jesus' Life and Teachings

The life of Jesus presents the ultimate demonstration of sacrifice. By His example and in His teachings He emphasized the need of giving up many things which most people consider important in order to accomplish a higher good. He also made it clear that we should offer, not only material gifts, but also our own selves to God as an expression of our repentance and commitment to Him.

We see that at the source of it all is the divine attribute of love. God loved so much that He gave His Son. The Son loved so much that He gave His life. The only way we can follow in the Path of Sacrifice is to share in that love. We will give acceptably only as we love.

Look again at the life of Jesus. Sacrifice characterized His whole experience. Mostly He gave Himself. He didn't spare His time. He didn't spare any effort. Selfishness was foreign to His character. He was always giving to those around Him: wisdom to those who wanted to learn, healing to those who suffered, freedom to those who were possessed of the devil, love to those who were lonely, and comfort to those who sorrowed.

For several weeks He had been trying to prepare the disciples for His arrest and death. It was such a different idea from theirs that they mentally refused to consider the possibility. So when He said, "Greater love hath no man than this," they really didn't know what He was talking about, but a few hours later they discovered His meaning as they saw Him die.

Not only did Jesus exemplify sacrifice by the life which He lived, His teachings emphasized the same thing. He tried to get His listeners to see the transitory nature of this world's goods, how relatively unimportant they are.

Remember the rich young man who came to Him? He said: "I have kept all of these commandments from my youth up." Jesus didn't argue with him. He was a good man as the world counts goodness. Jesus loved him and wanted him for His kingdom. So He told him: "Go and sell that thou hast, and give to the poor, and thou shalt have treasure in heaven: and come and follow me."

There is that command again, "Follow Me." And to the rich young man it turned out to be an Incredible Command, for it involved the sacrifice of his wealth. "He went away sorrowful: for he had great possessions." See Matthew 19:16-22.

Jesus told the story of the foolish rich man who said: "I am rich and increased with goods. I don't even have room to put up this year's crop. So I'll tear down my barns and build bigger ones, and say to my soul, 'Take thine ease, eat, drink, and be merry.'" And Jesus said: "Thou fool, this night thy soul shall be required of thee." See Luke 12:16-21.

In His Sermon on the Mount, Jesus said: "Lay up for yourselves treasures in heaven, where neither moth nor rust doth corrupt, and where thieves do not break through nor steal: for where your treasure is, there will your heart be also." Matthew 6:20, 21. He taught that what we have left, not what we give, is the measure of sacrifice. Our love for God should transcend our human relationships. Even the closest ties of family and loved ones may need to be sacrificed as we obey the command, "Follow Me."

Experience Teaches the Concept of Sacrifice

Some lessons of sacrifice we learn by observing our own experiences and the experiences of those around us. Actually we are introduced very early in life to the concept of sharing, giving in, and giving up.

Children learn, often rather painfully, that they must frequently yield something they want in order to get something they desire even more. These concepts become increasingly sophisticated as we grow older. Our parents and teachers and friends help us form a reasonable set of values. We progress from giving up playtime for the discipline of school to giving up bad habits of lifestyle for the building of healthy bodies. We learn to give up some of the things we would like to buy in order to have funds to purchase something we really need. God wants us to reach the condition where we will give up something of our own so someone else can have a better life.

The world around us is full of parables of sacrifice. Young athletes make incredible expenditures of time and undergo rigorous training in order to win at sports. Businessmen sacrifice their families, their health, and sometimes even their reputation in order to make money. People in the performing arts will go through amazing sacrifices in order to merit the applause of their audiences and the financial rewards they seek.

These are human goals and may be laudable in themselves. But I call them parables because they can teach us so much. If the individuals involved in these activities are willing to make great sacrifices for such goals as these, how much more should the child of God be not only willing, but eager, to make whatever sacrifice is necessary to obtain eternal life.

There are other very noble motives for sacrifice. Young men are sometimes called upon to sacrifice their lives for patriotism to country. We honor them.

When I was broadcasting in Manila before the war, I went into the office of the radio station's program director. While waiting to see him, my eye caught sight of a motto hanging on the wall. It said: "I complained because I had no shoes; and then I saw a man who had no feet." That motto was a blessing to me. I have never forgotten it.

Love, The Supreme Motive

Perhaps the easiest sacrifices we ordinarily make are those involving our loved ones. It's not hard for parents to give up things for their children. In families where love is alive, the mutual interplay of genuine affection involves constant sharing. It is beautiful to see. God wants us to extend this motive to include our entire attitude toward those around us. Most of all, He wants this to be the motive for all we do for him.

When our love for God becomes the biggest thing in our lives, more important than anything else or anyone else, then the sacrifices we are called upon to make come from a willing heart. They are done gladly, and such giving is acceptable to God.

Are you a little frightened when you think of what God might ask you to do? Perhaps you have seen your friends face difficult decisions. Some of them have turned away, fearing the sacrifice would be too great. Some have gone all the way with God. Their lives have become patterns of unselfish service. You envy them.

What if God wants you to give up a cherished career in order to go on some difficult errand for Him? What if He should require you to say goodbye to your family and move to a distant land? Could you turn away from someone you long to have as a life partner if that individual refuses to share your commitment to God? For some especially important project, could you make a financial sacrifice far beyond anything you have ever previously contemplated? Could you, if required, stand true to God, even if it cost your life?

My friend, do not tremble or turn away in despair at the solemn realization of what might be the result of giving yourself to God. Instead, listen to the voice of Jesus as He calls. It is not a harsh, commanding voice. It is not a severe, condemning voice. It is an earnest, entreating voice. And it promises that if you will follow in this Path of Sacrifice, as you follow you will grow stronger. You will feel more secure; your fears will turn to confidence and your doubts to praise.

Remember that Jesus never sends us on an untried trail. His feet have already traced the path. And it is in this path that you will see in all its beauty the amazing love that motivated our Saviour to lay down His life for you. As you follow with timid steps you will begin to assimilate a measure of that love. When it fills your heart, you will rejoice to make any sacrifice that is required.

Heavenly Father, our hearts are melted by your love in sending Your Son, and by His love in giving Himself for us. The small gifts we have to offer seem insignificant. The things we leave behind to follow Thee have lost their value in the light that shines from the cross. Teach us now to reflect Thy love to others. For we ask it in Jesus' name. Amen.

Chapter 14
"With His Stripes We Are Healed"

As we continue to trace the footsteps of Jesus in paths which led to His ultimate sacrifice, we consider once more the all-powering motivation which drove Him on. It was love. From the depths of His divine compassion flowed a fountain of love. During the final hours before His trial and conviction, Jesus directed this healing current to His disciples. His heart filled with a desire to make this a time they would never forget.

As He met with them in the upper room for the Passover supper, He made it clear to them that there was something different about this Passover. Instead of looking back, this Passover supper looked forward. Instead of representing the deliverance from Egypt, this one represented the deliverance from sin. Instead of merely foreshadowing the coming of the Messiah as the Lamb of God, it looked beyond to the second coming of Jesus as King of kings and Lord of lords.

But the most significant factor of all was the way Jesus felt that night. "Before the feast of the passover, when Jesus knew that his hour was come that he should depart out of this world unto the Father, having loved his own which were in the world, he loved them unto the end." John 13:1.

That is the setting for the original Lord's Supper. "Having loved his own . . . he loved them unto the end."

Jesus loved His own—even Judas. And He loved them despite their defects of character, despite their failure to understand His mission. Looking around on them, He must have shuddered just a little as He realized that He would leave on their shoulders the responsibility of carrying the gospel to the whole world!

One amazing fact made it all real. He loved them, without limit, unto the end. The same current of love that embraced the disciples in the upper room reached out to include all who witnessed the closing events of Jesus' life. It included the two thieves who were crucified with Him. It even included those who nailed Him to the cross.

To help us visualize the Calvary scene, will you join me as we consider three individuals who knew Jesus well? They are Nicodemus, Mary Magdalene, and Peter. We could choose many, but these three will characterize a complete spectrum of all the human family. Let's imagine that we are part of that milling crowd that has gathered at the place of crucifixion. We press our way through until we are quite close to the rise of the hill where the three crosses stand.

Jesus hangs on the center cross, the crown of thorns still in place as His head sags forward in agony. Our eyes drift slowly over the faces of others who are near the cross, pausing when we see someone we recognize, trying to imagine how he or she must be feeling. Are you a bit surprised to see the man called Nicodemus? He comes from the highest level of society. His credentials are impeccable. A very wealthy man, he is a specialist in Hebrew law. Dr. Nicodemus! A man greatly respected by his peers, he also commands the admiration of the entire nation. He is a member of the Sanhedrin. A genuine VIP. We recall his interview with Jesus by night.

Sometime early in Jesus' ministry, Nicodemus heard about Him. He felt strangely disturbed. Who is this Man? (Could it be that Nicodemus had been among that group of teachers and leaders who sat amazed in the temple when Jesus, a boy of twelve, asked and answered questions in dialogue with them?) In any event, what Nicodemus heard about Jesus made him uncomfortable. He felt attracted to Him and secretly admired Him. He took the only way he could figure out to talk to Jesus. He arranged for a clandestine meeting at night.

It turned out to be a fascinating conversation. Nicodemus began on what he considered safe ground. "We know that thou art a teacher come from God: for no man can do these miracles that thou doest, except God be with him." But Jesus knew what this man needed. Forsaking the philosophical approach, Jesus cut right through to the heart of truth: "Except a man be born again, he cannot see the kingdom of God."

This caught Nicodemus off guard. He had heard the new-birth symbolism used in describing converts to Judaism. But the implication that he, a leader in Israel, must be born again presented a disturbing concept. Gently Jesus opened to him this new world of spiritual thought.

During that conversation, Jesus gave him what has become our most beloved passage: "God so loved the world, that he gave his only begotten Son, that whosoever believeth in him should not perish, but have everlasting life." Nicodemus suddenly found himself talking with a divine Philosopher who gave him for the first time a real glimpse of the meaning of life. John 3:1-21.

How Nicodemus felt when he left the presence of Jesus we do not know. Subsequent events indicate that he must have been much impressed. At a later time when the Sanhedrin considered condemning Jesus, he spoke up and urged restraint. They turned on him and said: "Art thou also of Galilee? Search, and look: for out of Galilee ariseth no prophet." John 7:52. But his act of courage did postpone the capture of Jesus.

Now we find Nicodemus at the cross. We begin to realize that this is where everyone must come who would follow Christ. Our attention shifts to Mary Magdalene. We know more about her than about Nicodemus. Here is her story. She met Jesus in a most unusual circumstance. The rulers formed a plot to trap Jesus into making a statement they could use against Him with the Roman authorities. It was a frame-up.

One of the rulers, counting on the double standard and the connivance of his fellows to protect him, agreed to be discovered with this woman whose reputation was well known, and whom he deliberately seduced.[1] And then they dragged her into Jesus' presence. "We have caught her in adultery, taken in the very act. Moses said such should be stoned. What is your verdict?"

Jesus saw through their transparent plot immediately. He

took care of the momentary problem by stooping down and writing with His finger in the sand the grosser sins of those who were accusing this woman.[2] He lifted Himself up and said: "He that is without sin among you, let him first cast a stone at her."

He stooped again, continuing His writing. One after another, embarrassed and shamed, the accusers drifted away. When Jesus raised Himself again, He stood alone with Mary.

"Hath no man condemned thee?"

"No man, Lord."

"Neither do I condemn thee." Then He put the whole episode into the perspective of God's plan for saving men: "Go, and sin no more." See John 8:3-11.

Of her guilt there could be no question. Jesus neither ignored, nor condoned, nor excused her sin. He forgave. It would be a fine record if Mary had never sinned again. But it doesn't seem to be that way. There is good reason to feel that she was the sister of Martha and Lazarus, the one from whom Jesus cast seven devils. This might indicate that she had repeated bouts with sin. But eventually by the grace of Christ she overcame. The whole community stood amazed at the transformation of this woman with the shady reputation, who now loved to sit at Jesus' feet.

"Her sins, which are many, are forgiven; for she loved much," Jesus said. Luke 7:47. When she anointed His feet at Simon's feast and some complained about it, Jesus rebuked them. "Wheresoever this gospel shall be preached throughout the whole world, this also that she hath done shall be spoken of for a memorial of her." Mark 14:9.

Now our eyes focus on a man whom we recognize at once. It's Peter. He looks like a broken man. He cannot take his eyes off Jesus. Most of us can identify easily with him. Always quick to speak, impetuous of action, impulsive of thought, he reminds us of ourselves. And yet he had a flair for leadership, a man of strong character, one of Jesus' most effective disciples.

One time he got Jesus in trouble with the Internal Revenue people! They asked, "Doesn't your Master pay this tax?"

"Yes, of course He pays," said Peter—a tax which Jesus, as a religious leader, was exempt from paying.

When Jesus returned and heard about the conversation, what did He do? "Now, Peter, you go back and tell those people the facts; set them straight!" No. It is really a beautiful story. Jesus performed one of His amazing miracles—the coin in the fish's mouth—to save Peter's face! Matthew 17:24-27.

At the Lord's Supper, when Jesus approached Peter with a basin and a towel, His impetuous disciple declared, "Thou shalt never wash my feet."

"If I wash thee not, thou hast no part with me."

Peter made a full about-face. "Not my feet only, but also my hands and my head." John 13:6-9. Here was a man that wavered between total commitment and tragic failure. A little later he said to Jesus: "I will lay down my life for thy sake." John 13:37. But in just a few hours he denied his Lord.

Consider that picture. Jesus, standing on trial in the high priest's palace. Just a few feet away, in the courtyard in the shadows, cowering over the fire with the servants, we find Peter. He has just sworn and cursed to emphasize his declaration that he never knew the Man. Meanwhile Jesus stands as witnesses hurl their false accusations at Him. The Jewish rulers sit in judgment, vengeful, thirsting for His life. The fate of the whole human race trembles in the balance.

At that moment, "The Lord turned." the record says, "and looked upon Peter." Luke 22:61. Peter saw no bitterness, no anger, no condemnation in that look. Only a poignant mixture of love and disappointment. It broke Peter's heart.[3] That look of love planted there a seed of genuine, total conversion that bore a noble harvest a few weeks later at Pentecost.

My friend, do you find yourself anywhere in the pictures of these three individuals? Is there anything in Nicodemus's confused intellectualism that awakens a response in your thinking? How about Mary? Jesus forgave Mary. That means He can forgive you. Peter? Are you sometimes impulsive, speaking up too quickly, failing at the moment of test?

If you find yourself in any of these pictures, you'll be glad you have joined Peter, Mary, and Nicodemus at the foot of the cross. What are the emotions in the hearts of these individuals? How do they react as they see Jesus hanging on that cross?

How do you react?

Perhaps the least surprised of all is Nicodemus. He remembers what Jesus said during that late-night visit. "As Moses lifted up the serpent in the wilderness, even so must the Son of man be lifted up." Now he is looking at that Son of man, lifted up on the cross. Now he understands. Here Nicodemus makes his first public confession of faith in Jesus. He comes forward and uses his wealth to buy spices to embalm His body.

Mary stands at the cross, looking at this One whom she thought was going to be her King. She had heard Him say He was going to die, so she had bought the ointment to use for His burial. When she witnessed the triumphal entry, her heart had thrilled, and she thought, "He isn't going to die after all. He's going to set up His kingdom." So she had poured it on His feet at Simon's feast. Now she stands at the foot of the cross and watches, weeping, as the Man who saved her life lays down His own. She is devastated.

Peter is still here. As he sees Jesus hanging on the cross there floods into his mind the bitter memory of those few hours before, when with vehemence and vulgarity he had denied that he had ever known this Man. Now Peter, in an agony of remorse, sees Jesus lay down His.

My friend, come closer to the foot of the cross, with Nicodemus and Mary and Peter. You stand there with all the others, numbed by the unfolding tragedy. Many in the crowd have been comforted by Jesus, healed by His touch, saved by His message. Now all are witnesses of His ultimate sacrifice. All can see that His love has no limit.

This is where you inevitably must come when you follow Jesus—to the cross. And as you stand there with these others and you look upon Him hanging there, somehow all the other people fade. You seem to stand alone. And you sob: "He dies for me!" This becomes the most important experience of your life.

I want to join Nicodemus, Mary, and Peter at the foot of the cross just now. I want to say to this Man who dies for me, "I'll follow. I don't know what it means, what it will cost, or where it will lead. But you have called me. I will obey."

Will you join me now at the foot of the cross? With Peter,

116 INCREDIBLE COMMAND

Nicodemus, Mary, and the others? If you will, just bow your head right where you are now, and give your life to Him.

> When I survey the wondrous cross
> On which the Prince of glory died,
> My richest gain I count but loss,
> And pour contempt on all my pride.
>
> See, from His head, His hands, His feet,
> Sorrow and love flow mingled down;
> Did e'er such love and sorrow meet?
> Or thorns compose so rich a crown?
>
> Since I, who was undone and lost,
> Have pardon through His name and word,
> Forbid it, then, that I should boast,
> Save in the cross of Christ, my Lord.
>
> Were the whole realm of nature mine,
> That were a tribute far too small;
> Love so amazing, so divine,
> Demands my life, my soul, my all.[4]

Heavenly Father, we stand at the foot of the cross, where Jesus, offers the ultimate sacrifice. Our hearts are broken; we cry, "He dies for me!" We accept His command, "Follow Me!" And we say, "Lord, we'll follow." Please accept this commitment. Take our lives. Make them over. Use us to complete Your plan. Help us to follow You all the way into Your heavenly kingdom. For we ask it, Jesus, in Your name. Amen.

---

1. *The Desire of Ages*, p. 566.
2. *Ibid.*, p. 461.
3. *Ibid.*, pp. 712, 713.
4. Isaac Watts

The Path of Satisfaction

"Looking unto Jesus the author and finisher of our faith; who for the joy that was set before him endured the cross, despising the shame, and is set down at the right hand of the throne of God." Hebrews 12:2.

"It will be seen that He who is infinite in wisdom could devise no plan for our salvation except the sacrifice of His Son. The compensation for this sacrifice is the joy of peopling the earth with ransomed beings, holy, happy, and immortal. The result of the Saviour's conflict with the powers of darkness is joy to the redeemed, redounding the glory of God throughout eternity. And such is the value of the soul that the Father is satisfied with the price paid; and Christ Himself, beholding the fruits of His great sacrifice, is satisfied."—*The Great Controversy,* p. 652.

Chapter 15
Satisfaction Guaranteed

Throughout these pages we have been talking about Jesus. We have noticed that when He came to this earth and began His life of service, He drew about Him a group of people with whom He would leave the awesome task of giving the gospel to all the world. And as He called them, He said: "Follow Me!"

This is an Incredible Command. It is incredible because it comes to human beings who under ordinary circumstances would never have either the opportunity or the possibility of following such a Leader.

You have traced the footsteps where Jesus walked: through the Paths of Simplicity, Supplication, Self-Denial, Service, Suffering, and Sacrifice. At the close of the previous chapter, standing at the foot of the cross, you made the decision to accept the command and follow Him. And now you want to consider the final path where Jesus walked. It is the Path of Satisfaction. Our chapter title is "Satisfaction Guaranteed."

Perhaps the finest picture we have in preview of what Jesus would do when He came to earth is recorded by the prophet Isaiah in the fifty-third chapter of his book. We refer to it often, especially at the Christmas season. Many of its words are included in the magnificent oratorio *Messiah*. He was "a man of sorrows, and acquainted with grief: and we hid as it were our faces from him; . . . We did esteem him stricken, smitten of God, and afflicted. . . . He is brought as a lamb to the slaughter." But sometimes we forget that a little farther down in that same chapter we come to verse eleven. Here it says triumphantly:

"He shall see the travail of his soul, and shall be satisfied."

How sad it would be if we left ourselves with the opinion that Jesus had nothing but suffering, mental anguish, disappointment, rejection, and discouragement during the whole of His earthly experience. Rather, Jesus had a large measure of satisfaction throughout His ministry. And though He was "a man of sorrows, and acquainted with grief," yet He lived a life that knew its great moments of joy. Consider some of the things in which Jesus found satisfaction.

He did not feel the need of the material things that so many people seek. Have you ever stopped to think how much of your time is spent in planning, working, and searching for *things*? It matters little whether we are talking about shoelaces or houses. We plan, we save, we go through mental and fiscal gymnastics in order to add more *things* to those we already possess—and we have convinced ourselves that we need them.

Now I don't argue against that. Certainly we do have multiple needs. And yet, Jesus found it possible to live without that constant demand on His mind. He never felt that He must acquire more in order to be happy. This very freedom from anxiety for *things* gave Him a wonderful satisfaction.

Jesus lived a life of inner peace. How much of our anguish is caused by the mistakes we make! Not only do the mistakes themselves exact a penalty, but there is always the sense of remorse, bitterness, and wishing we hadn't done it. We all of us understand this. Jesus never experienced it. For Himself, He had no need to feel repentant, no remorse, no agony for mistakes. That inner peace goes beyond what we can imagine. Yet Christ, through His forgiveness, through His compassion, through His longsuffering, has promised that we, too, may enjoy it.

We find this life of inner peace reflected in Jesus' attitude toward those around Him and toward the circumstances in which He found Himself. Consider the story of Jesus sleeping in the boat on Galilee. The disciples, who had spent their lives on that sea, found themselves in difficulties they could no longer control. Fear turned to panic. Then, in a flash of lightning they suddenly noticed the sleeping, peaceful face of Jesus.

Desperate, they awakened Him. How could He be asleep!

"Master, carest thou not that we perish?"

Jesus simply stood in that tossing boat, then He turned and said to the winds and waves, "Peace, be still." The disciples shook their heads in disbelief. "What manner of man is this, that even the wind and the sea obey him?" Mark 4:36-41. That inner peace was something they didn't understand.

Jesus knew the thrill of accomplishment. When we read about His miracles, about the success of His teachings in the lives of the people, our attention is always concentrated on the individuals involved. The sick who were healed, the blind who could see, those possessed with demons who had their souls set free—how could we overlook the fact that these experiences must have brought an immense joy to Jesus Himself? Certainly He was not immune to that emotion.

Jesus also rejoiced to see transformation of character. Remember Zacchaeus, the man who tried to keep out of sight in the tree? Jesus spotted him. "Zacchaeus, make haste, and come down; for to day I must abide at thy house."

Zacchaeus took Him home. Outside many in the crowd mumbled and grumbled because He had gone to eat with another one of those publicans and sinners. But what did Jesus say? "This day is salvation come to this house." Luke 19:2-9. His heart thrilled to see the change in Zacchaeus's character.

Jesus wanted the disciples to look back on these satisfying experiences and to share in His joy. We think of the night before His crucifixion, as He talked with the disciples while walking from the upper room to the Garden of Gethsemane. Although they did not understand the significance of His coming trial, they had some sense of foreboding because of what they had heard Jesus say. But Jesus' concern was for these men.

And what did He tell them on that night? "These things have I spoken unto you, that my joy might remain in you, and that your joy might be full." And the same night, a little later, He said: "Ye shall be sorrowful, but your sorrow shall be turned into joy." John 15:11; 16:20.

But, of course, the ultimate fulfillment of Isaiah's prophecy, "He shall see of the travail of his soul, and shall be satisfied," will be realized when Jesus comes again. Then He will keep His promise: "That where I am, there ye may be also." We can only faintly imagine the satisfaction that will come to Jesus when He presents the saved of all the ages to His heavenly Father in the kingdom. So should we not be exultant that Jesus says: "Follow Me in the Path of Satisfaction"?

Christians—The World's Happiest People

Christians ought to be the happiest people in the world. We have so much going for us. We ought to enjoy all these things that Jesus enjoyed. We ought to have the feeling that there is great happiness, great hope, great courage! We should remember that every trial will bring in exchange a measure of satisfaction and happiness.

We can have the peace of mind that Jesus had. We may not know it to the same degree, for our trust is limited to our experience and our faith. But the promise is for us: "The peace of God, which passeth all understanding, shall keep your hearts and minds through Christ Jesus." Philippians 4:7.

In the book of Ecclesiastes, Solomon, the wise man, tells us that we ought to enjoy the little things in life every day. He points out that we work, we struggle, and we should enjoy the fruits of our labors. Every day good things happen to us. We should be alert to recognize these blessings and be happy in the pleasure they bring. Following Jesus in the Path of Satisfaction keeps us in the attitude of praise. God is good. He wants us to find real joy as we participate in what He promises to do for us and in what He asks us to do for Him.

Take the question of service. During a Week of Spiritual Emphasis in one of our colleges, a young woman came into the office where I met with students who wanted counseling.

"I don't have a problem," she said. "I just wanted to share something with you."

Her eyes were shining. She told me how she had joined a witnessing team in a nearby town the previous Sabbath afternoon. They had stepped up to the door of a home, and the woman who answered their knock very hesitantly had let them in. After they had talked for a little while, her forbidding attitude changed to one of tears and rejoicing. Before they left she had invited them to come and visit her again.

You should have seen the face of this student as she told me the story. You cannot buy that kind of satisfaction.

As I think back over my ministry, there have been a number of things that have made me very happy. Many of my most enjoyable experiences came from my years of radio broadcasting. As a boy I was fascinated with radio. When I entered the ministry I could hardly wait for a chance to get on the air.

Well, the chance came earlier than I had expected. The brethren approved a modest broadcasting schedule in the church where I served as pastor. Soon, however, we took our first overseas assignment and left for Japan. Christian radio broadcasts there were impossible.

About a year before Pearl Harbor we were transferred from Japan to the Philippines. A visit to the radio station in Manila revealed that they would welcome a Christian broadcast—for a price, of course. The brethren encouraged me by giving me a budget for a weekly program. After we started, I approached the management of the radio station and persuaded them to let me have free time for two other regular programs.

I developed one broadcast for children called "Storytime with Uncle Paul." This program went on the air each Sunday morning at eight o'clock. We invited children to join "Uncle Paul's Story Club" and sent each a little button to wear on his jacket. Each child also received a membership card that said, "This is to certify that you are a member of Uncle Paul's Story Club."

The children responded enthusiastically. Soon we had 600 club members. Intrigued, the radio station made this broadcast a regular Sunday morning feature, even though we paid nothing for the time.

One Sunday morning a few months later, I arrived at the station in time for our program. Imagine my surprise to discover that a group of entertainers with a combo was in the studio, preparing to go on the air at our time! An ambitious salesman had assumed the station would welcome a sponsor instead of a sustaining program and had sold our time to an advertiser.

Having heard nothing about it, I felt quite upset, to put it mildly. I didn't know what to do or say. The station announcer on duty that morning took charge and called the program director to clear it all up. The director had not been informed of the changes. There were only a few moments until air time. The director made his decision without hesitation. "Mr. Eldridge goes on as usual." And so the station turned down the money and let me go on to talk to the children.

God blessed those programs. They were exciting. I got a great deal of satisfaction out of preparing and broadcasting them. But that is not the end of the story. About thirty-five years later I visited one of our churches in the Chicago area. A Filipino woman stepped up to me. She smiled and said: "I was one of your children in your Uncle Paul's stories in the Philippines." Don't you think that gave me a real burst of satisfaction?

After the war, we returned to Japan. A new era of radio broadcasting began in that country. We were able to get on the air with the Voice of Prophecy in Japanese. How thrilled we were! Yet we had no way of knowing how far-reaching the result would be.

A number of years later when we were here in the United States on furlough, Mrs. Eldridge and I found ourselves one Friday evening in a hotel in the city of Tampa, Florida. We didn't know anyone in the city. I picked up the telephone directory and searched for the listing of the Seventh-day Adventist church. When I found the number, I dialed it and the pastor answered. As soon as I had introduced myself, he said: "Good! We would like to have you take the service tomorrow." I agreed.

The next morning we found the Tampa church. As I signed the guest book, the woman who greeted us noticed that we were from Japan and said: "Oh, we have a Japanese lady here. I'm sure you would like to meet her."

She went inside the sanctuary and soon came out, accompanied by this woman. She turned out to be one of the secretaries in the Sabbath School. She had married an American serviceman during the occupation. When we were introduced, her face beamed, and she said: "My first contact with Seventh-day Adventists came when I lay sick with tuberculosis in a hospital in Nagano. I listened to your radio program!" What a thrill it was to meet her. The Lord let me have another satisfying bonus that comes as a result of serving him.

One time at our Voice of Prophecy offices in Tokyo, an inspector from the postal department showed up. He said he had been sent to trace a letter. Well, we received a steady stream of letters. It took several days to process them. Each letter had to be checked carefully. Some were new enrollments. Some were lesson sheets being returned for grading. Some were questions about personal problems.

The inspector said: "We have had a request from someone who sent you a letter. He is wondering if his letter failed to arrive since he has had no reply."

Our girls who processed the mail were a little nervous. They started leafing through the stacks of letters. And sure enough, they found the letter in question. It had arrived about two days before. The inspector was satisfied. He had just wanted to make sure the letter had been delivered.

But we began to wonder. "What is so important in that letter that the writer became upset when he didn't receive a reply within twenty-four hours?" We opened the letter and read it through. It obviously came from a very distressed person. The letter was from a man who had listened to one of my broadcasts in which I had given answers to some personal questions that had been sent in. He had heard me say that I would respond to anyone who wanted such counsel.

In his letter he had included a telephone number with the request that I call him right away. Since he had not received a call as soon as he had expected, he had requested the post office department to trace his letter. You can be sure that with this background, I wasted no time in getting on the phone and calling his number. He answered so quickly that it seemed as though he had been waiting for the phone to ring.

He wanted to have a personal talk with me, so we quickly agreed on a time later that day when it would be convenient for him to come to my office. Here was someone who was not a Christian. He had never been to a Christian church. He had never looked inside a Bible. But he had listened to my program and thought I might be able to give him help.

When he came to my office his distress was obvious. He told me a long, sad story. He lived in a small town not far from the city of Nagoya. There he had been employed in the post office. An attractive young lady worked at the desk next to his. ince he had a lovely wife and a son about eight years old, he had originally felt no more than professional interest in this girl. But as time went on, the law of propinquity took over. Acquaintance turned to friendship, and friendship to infatuation.

Soon it became a full-blown affair. The girl, of course, wanted him to divorce his wife and marry her. However, he still loved his wife. In order to assure herself that the man would marry her, the girl talked him into moving to Tokyo with her, where she had a job offer. She assured him that she could go to work right away and support them until he could find a job. So he gave up his job, left his wife and son, and moved to Tokyo.

But he felt miserable. He missed his family. He was mortified to think he was living on the income of the young woman with no immediate prospects of a job. While mulling over his feelings of remorse, he had heard our radio program and had turned to me for help.

We talked for a long time. Plainly he still felt a very deep affection for his wife. He also keenly regretted what he had done to her. Naturally I urged him to part company with the young woman, return home, and see if his wife would be willing to take him back. I explained to him that from a moral standpoint she did not have to let him return, but she just might be willing to do that. He decided to make the break and try a reconciliation with his wife. When he left my office I had no idea what the outcome would be. I knew it would not be easy to break with the young woman who had come to love him and desperately wanted him to become her husband.

Several months passed. I had almost forgotten the incident. New Year's time came. In Japan this is the biggest holiday of the year. In the older Japanese tradition, a person was considered to be one year old at birth and a year older on each succeeding New Year's Day. So the beginning of the New Year is occasion for nationwide celebration. For the first three days the country practically comes to a standstill, except for the bustle of people going about visiting each other!

On the second day of that New Year our doorbell rang. When I opened the door I saw standing there a Japanese family: a man, his wife, and an eight-year-old boy. I looked at them for a long moment before I realized that this man was the one who had been in my office! Suddenly the picture became clear. The man had gone back to his wife and son, and they had accepted him! The man said, "We have come to thank you for helping us get our family together again."

I invited them in. After we had visited for a while, we had prayer together—a new experience for them. Then he asked, "How can I get a Bible?" Needless to say, we were more than glad to give him one. When it came time to leave, my wife joined me, and we had our picture taken with the family just outside our home. The man's wife had tears in her eyes—tears of joy.

There isn't any salary, there isn't any gift, there isn't any bonus that can bring the kind of satisfaction I felt that day.

My friend, your decision to accept the Incredible Command to follow Jesus has brought joy in heaven. God wants you to share this joy, even though your path may still take you through the troubles and difficulties of this world. These small satisfactions along the way are His method of assuring you that the final triumphs are just ahead.

When Jesus says, "Follow Me!" He doesn't mean just following Him to the foot of the cross. He means following on past the cross to the crown. That's when your joy will be full. You, with Him, will see the travail of your soul and will be satisfied.

The author of Hebrews has put it all into perspective: "Wherefore seeing we also are compassed about with so great a cloud of witnesses, let us lay aside every weight, and the sin which doth so easily beset us, and let us run with patience the race that is set before us, looking unto Jesus the author and finisher of our faith; who for the joy that was set before him endured the cross, despising the shame, and is set down at the right hand of the throne of God." Hebrews 12:1, 2.

When Jesus says, "Follow Me," we walk not only in the Paths of Simplicity, Supplication, Self-Denial, Service, Suffering, and Sacrifice, but also toward the joyful rewards He has promised here in this life, and in the life to come—the Path of Satisfaction.

"Come, Follow Me!"
I heard the Master's voice, and turned to see
For whom this invitation had been given;
"Whose heart so pure," I thought, "whose life so fine
To merit thus the Master's gracious call?"
No one was there. I turned again, and saw
That it was I to whom the Master spoke:
"Thy sins I will forgive, thy doubts dispel,
Thy weakness strengthen, and thy faith reward.
Come thou, and Follow Me!"

"Come, Follow Me!"
The Master stands and beckons as He calls.
I see ahead the path where duty lies.
The way is rough, the task demands more skill,
More wisdom, more great courage than I know.
"Not this road, Lord!" I pray, "and not this task!"
The Master answers, "Fear thou not to come—
My feet shall try the trail; thy burden's weight
Is measured by the strength I will bestow.
Come thou, and Follow Me!"

"Come, Follow Me!"
The voice is sweet, yet like an organ's tone
It sweeps across the shining crystal sea
Where stand in solemn joy the saints of God
Before the glory gates of Paradise.
The Master calls each name, and every cross
Becomes a victor's golden crown. Then as
His nail-pierced hand lays hold of heaven's gate
And swings it open wide, the Master says,
"Come thou, and Follow Me!"[1]

---

1. Paul H. Eldridge